In Love
with a
PERSON
I'VE NEVER MET

7 BIBLICAL PRINCIPLES FOR DISCOVERING TRUE LOVE

JEREMY SANFORD

Copyright © 2025 by Jeremy Sanford

All rights reserved. No part of this book may be reproduced, stored in a retrieval system, or transmitted in any form or by any means—electronic, mechanical, photocopying, recording, scanning, or otherwise—without the prior written permission of the publisher, except in the case of brief quotations embodied in reviews and articles.

Scripture quotations are taken from the Holy Bible, King James Version (KJV). Public Domain.

Some names and identifying details have been changed to protect the privacy of individuals.

Published in the United States by:
Jeremy Sanford Inc.
Jackson, MS

ISBN: 979-8-9931036-0-0

This book is a work of nonfiction. The names, stories, and circumstances are based on the author's personal experiences and beliefs. Any resemblance to actual persons, living or dead, outside of these accounts is purely coincidental.

Printed in the United States of America

Acknowledgements

First, I give glory and honor to my Lord and Savior, Jesus Christ. Without Him, I would not be here. He saved my life, changed my heart, and called me into a purpose greater than myself. Every word in this book is the overflow of His grace and goodness.

To my parents—thank you for being the foundation that shaped me. Dad, you have been my greatest coach and biggest supporter from the very beginning. From bringing me lunches at school to getting up in the middle of the night to fix a flat tire, you have always been there. You taught me perseverance, sacrifice, and what it looks like for a father to love without limits. Mom, you have been my anchor in God. Your wisdom, prayers, and spiritual counsel have made me the man of God I am today. I would not be preaching the gospel, nor walking in this calling, without your guidance. You gave me roots, and I will always honor you for that.

To my wife, LaTresha—the star of this story. You are the love I searched for and the blessing God entrusted to me. The journey to find you was not easy, but it was worth every step. You cheer me on before every sermon and every speech, and you are the heartbeat of this love story. You make me better, and this book is as much yours as it is mine.

To my son, Jeremiah—you are my heart, my joy, and the reason I smile every day. I never knew I could love a child the way I love you. You inspire me with your strength and your ability to push past barriers even at such a young age. This book is for you, to show you that with faith and perseverance, nothing is impossible.

To my brother, Micah—my day one. Only 10 months separate us, but in many ways, we are as close as twins. You've always been willing to do anything for me, and you will forever be my first best friend.

To my sister-in-law, Kayla—you are truly the best sister-in-law I could have asked for. You've been a blessing to our family, and I thank God for you.

To my immediate and extended family—your love, support, and sacrifice have shaped who I am. Each of you is a thread in the fabric of my life, and I carry you in my heart always.

To my pastor, Bishop Robert N. Fortson Sr. —thank you for teaching me what God requires: a life of holiness. You instilled in me principles that are a staple for my life and my ministry.

To my church family—you have walked with me from the very beginning. You've prayed for me, supported me, and celebrated every milestone along the way. Your love means the world to me.

To my father-in-law, thank you for being a sounding board, a man of wisdom, and an example I can look up to. To my mother-in-law, your strength and virtue reflect the heart of God, and I am grateful to walk this journey with your prayers and support.

To Heather Monahan and Dr. Rhonda Mattox—thank you for your mentorship, your coaching, and your reminders that my calling is great and more is always possible.

Finally, to every person who has ever believed in me, encouraged me, or invested in me—this book would not exist without you. Your words, your love, and your faith have carried me through, and I pray these pages pour back into you as much as you have poured into me.

This book is dedicated to LaTresha and Jeremiah.
My forever love, my legacy.

Contents

Chapter 1	Dear Soul Mate	1
Chapter 2	The Promise	9
Chapter 3	When Did Singleness Become a Disease?	19
Chapter 4	Single vs. Unmarried	27
Chapter 5	Maximizing Your Potential	35
Chapter 6	My Singleness Has an Expiration Date	43
Chapter 7	The License to Hunt	51
Chapter 8	Attraction Psychology	59
Chapter 9	The Power of Visualization	67
Chapter 10	The List	73
Chapter 11	Are they out of my League?	79
Chapter 12	Ask sooner	85
Chapter 13	Cleanse Yourself	89
Chapter 14	Love before First Sight	95
Chapter 15	Let The Guns Blaze	103
Chapter 16	The War Within	109
Chapter 17	Love worth Fighting for	117
Chapter 18	A Perfect Match…Kinda	125
Chapter 19	The Single Person's Anthem	133
Chapter 20	Ageless Love	141
Chapter 21	When Destinies Collide	147
Chapter 22	I Thought I Did, But I Don't	155
Chapter 23	The Flight That Changed My Life	161
Chapter 24	God Saved the Best for Last	169
Chapter 25	Living the Dream I Prayed For	175
7 Biblical Principles for Finding True Love		181

CHAPTER

1

Dear Soul Mate

There is more hunger for love and appreciation in this world than for bread.

MOTHER TERESA
Winner of the Nobel Peace Prize

I have a confession.
I think I'm falling in love with someone I've never met.

Sounds crazy, right? Who does that? Who risks their heart on a dream? On a person whose name, face, and story are still hidden?

But stay with me. Because this isn't about obsession. It isn't about chasing shadows. It's about something far more radical—faith.

Faith that love isn't an accident of timing, but a divine appointment. Faith that the person God designed for you isn't just "out there" somewhere, but already written into your story. Faith that before you ever meet them, you can begin preparing your heart, your habits, and your future to welcome them.

Most people think love starts when two people finally meet. I believe it starts much earlier. It starts now—with the way you live, the way you wait, the way you prepare.

And here's the hard truth: too many singles waste this season wishing instead of becoming. They wait for love to change their life instead of realizing that how they live today will shape the love they find tomorrow.

This book is about breaking that cycle.
It's about learning to fall in love with a person you haven't met by first falling in love with God's plan for your life, your purpose, and your preparation.

Because the truth is: you don't attract what you want. You attract what you are.

The Radical Idea

When you saw the title of this book, you may have raised an eyebrow: *In Love with a Person I've Never Met?*
At first glance, it feels extreme. A little wild. Maybe even absurd.

But think about it. People risk their hearts all the time for someone they barely know. They swipe on dating apps, trust online profiles, go on blind dates arranged by friends—all in the hope that love might be waiting on the other side. Sometimes it works. Sometimes it's disappointing. And sometimes, it ends in heartbreak.

We live in a world where love feels more like rolling dice than following destiny. And in that kind of world, the idea of loving someone you haven't met yet sounds risky, almost foolish.

But what if the risk wasn't in waiting for them… but in failing to prepare for them?

That's what I'm really talking about. Falling in love with someone you haven't met isn't about obsession, fantasy, or infatuation. It's about choosing faith—a faith that sees beyond the present moment into the future God has already prepared. It's about trusting that your spouse is not just a possibility but a divine appointment.

And if that's true, then love can—and must—begin before you meet them.

Why Faith Matters in Love

Faith is more than belief. It's vision. It's the ability to see what isn't visible yet and live as though it already exists. Scripture tells us:

> *"Faith is the substance of things hoped for,*
> *the evidence of things not seen."*
> —Hebrews 11:1

That means you can begin to prepare today for a relationship you haven't stepped into yet.
You can sow seeds of love before you know the soil it will grow in.
You can decide to become the kind of person who will attract, honor, and cherish the spouse God has written into your future.

This is why so many singles miss it. They wait passively—scrolling through profiles, hoping someone will appear—when what they should be doing is living intentionally. Love doesn't start when you meet "the one." Love starts with the decisions you make when no one is watching.

If you want a marriage filled with kindness, respect, and generosity, then you must practice kindness, respect, and generosity right now. If you want a relationship rooted in faith, then faith must already be rooted in you.

The way you live today is a preview of the love you'll experience tomorrow.

The World's Version vs. God's Version

Let's be honest: the world has cheapened love.
It markets love as chemistry, butterflies, romance, and attraction. It packages it as entertainment—a plotline in movies, a hashtag on social media, a song on the radio.

But those feelings, while exciting, don't last. They fade. They shift. They change.

Real love isn't about goosebumps or heart flutters. It's about commitment. It's about covenant. It's about building something that lasts through storms.

That's why so many relationships collapse—they were built on sand instead of rock. Conditional love says: *I'll stay as long as you meet my expectations.* But unconditional love says: *I'll stay even when you don't.*

Think about Jesus. He gave His life for us—not because we could ever pay Him back, not because we had anything to offer, but simply because He loved. That's the model. That's the standard.

And if we want marriages that endure, we must build them on that same kind of love.

Seeing Love Through New Lenses

Close your eyes for a moment and imagine the person of your dreams. You can probably picture them—how they look, how they carry themselves, maybe even how they'd laugh at your jokes.

But here's the reality: looks change. Bodies change. Circumstances change.

If your love is rooted in what is temporary, it will crumble when time does its work. But if your love is rooted in who a person truly is—their character, their spirit, their values—then that love can endure any season.

True love isn't about *what they bring to you*; it's about *who they are when life tests them*.

The spouse God has for you isn't meant to complete you—they're meant to complement the wholeness you've already built in Him. Which means your preparation now is critical.

Preparing Before the Meeting

Here's the secret: you don't wait until you meet them to start preparing. You prepare in advance.

That means:

- **Building character** when no one is watching.
- **Living with integrity** in your friendships and family.
- **Sowing love generously**—because Scripture says we reap what we sow.
- **Healing from past pain** so you don't drag old wounds into a new relationship.

If you want to build a love story that inspires others, you can't start later. You must start now.

Because preparation isn't wasted—it's investment. And the spouse you're believing for deserves your best version, not your leftover effort.

The Cost of Not Preparing

Let's be real: marriages don't fall apart on the wedding day. They fall apart because of years of neglect, unhealed wounds, selfish choices, and poor preparation.

If you don't cultivate discipline in your single season, you won't magically gain it in marriage. If you don't practice faithfulness now, a ring won't make you faithful later. If you don't heal now, your spouse won't fix you later.

That's why loving a person you've never met is so powerful. It shifts your mindset from passive waiting to active preparation. It makes you accountable. It makes you intentional. It reminds you that your choices today aren't just about you—they're about your future family, your future children, your future legacy.

The Invitation

If you're reading this, it's because you desire something more than casual love. You're hungry for something deeper—something God-centered, purposeful, and lasting.

I want to invite you on a journey. This book isn't just about finding someone. It's about becoming someone. It's about falling in love not only with your future spouse but with the process of preparation, the beauty of purpose, and the God who designed both.

Along the way, you'll be challenged to shift your perspective, confront your assumptions, and embrace the season you're in right now.

Because the truth is, this isn't just about *waiting for love*. It's about *living in love*.

Show Love Now

You don't have to wait until you're married to live out love. You can start practicing today.

Love your family. Love your friends. Love your coworkers. Love strangers who can't pay you back. Volunteer. Give. Serve.

Love isn't something you switch on when you meet the right person. It's something you live out daily.

And here's the biblical principle: *Whatever you sow, you will reap.* If you sow selfishness now, you'll reap conflict later. If you sow generosity now, you'll reap richness later.

So don't wait. Begin building the marriage you dream of—through your daily actions, attitudes, and disciplines.

The Foundation of Faith

At the core of all of this is faith. Faith that God sees you. Faith that God knows your desires. Faith that He hasn't forgotten you.

The enemy will whisper that you're behind, overlooked, unworthy, or broken. But God says otherwise. God says you are chosen, loved, and called. He says your steps are ordered. He says your story is already written.

The choice is simple: will you live in fear and impatience, or will you walk in faith and preparation?

My Confession Again

So yes—I'll say it again.
I'm falling in love with someone I've never met.

Not because I've lost my mind, but because I've found my faith.
Not because I'm obsessed with an idea, but because I'm committed to preparation.
Not because I'm lonely, but because I believe in legacy.

And I believe you can do the same.

Scriptural Reflection

> *"Love never fails. But where there are prophecies, they will cease; where there are tongues, they will be stilled; where there is knowledge, it will pass away."*
>
> —1 Corinthians 13:8

Love is not a trend. It's not a fleeting feeling. It's the one thing that endures forever. As you walk through this season, let your faith in love—God's love and the love He has prepared for you—be your anchor. Because what He ordains, no season, no delay, and no obstacle can destroy.

CHAPTER 2

The Promise

For every promise, there is a price to pay.

JIM ROHN
Self-made multimillionaire, Author, and Motivational speaker

Love doesn't begin on the wedding day. It doesn't begin the moment you exchange vows or walk down the aisle. And it certainly doesn't begin with a ring.

Love—the kind that endures, protects, and transforms—starts with a promise.

Not the kind spoken under lights or sealed with a kiss, but the private kind. The quiet kind. The kind whispered in prayer, forged in faith, and lived out in the spaces no one sees.

So, I make a promise to a woman I haven't even met yet. Yes, her. The girl of my dreams. The future wife I haven't laid eyes on.

I make her this promise: *I will prepare.*

The Myth of Effortless Love

There's a dangerous myth circulating in today's culture—and many have bought into it. It's the idea that great marriages are natural, effortless, and easy. That finding "the one" is like striking gold, and from there, everything flows without resistance.

But ask anyone in a thriving marriage and they'll tell you: **great love isn't found—it's formed.**

A strong, lasting marriage is the result of spiritual, emotional, and relational preparation. It's not about luck. It's about lifestyle. You can't have a kingdom marriage with a casual mentality. You can't expect marital success if you refuse to train for it in your single season.

Preparation is the price. And the earlier you pay it, the greater the return.

Childhood Habits, Adult Consequences

Let's dive deeper. Most of us walk into adult relationships with childhood habits, often unaware that we've brought baggage from homes we never fully healed from.

If your father only showed love through provision—food, shelter, and financial security—you may find yourself replicating that same pattern. Providing, but never expressing. Doing, but never saying. Present in body, but absent in affection.

On the other hand, if your mother nurtured you with kindness, warmth, and openness, you may long for that same level of emotional intimacy and vulnerability in your romantic connections.

Neither is "wrong"—but both must be understood.

Because **awareness creates the capacity for transformation.**

Before we prepare to love someone else well, we must reflect on what we learned about love in our earliest years. Some of those lessons were beautiful. Others were broken. And if we're honest, we've repeated them more times than we'd like to admit.

Reflection: What Did You Learn About Love?

Lessons that must be released:

- Name-calling during conflict
- Physical violence as a response to frustration
- Dishonesty or manipulation
- Harboring grudges
- Generalizations about gender ("All men are dogs," "Women can't be trusted")

Lessons worth reinforcing:

- Respecting women and elders
- Speaking love with words
- Quick forgiveness
- Expressing gratitude
- Keeping promises
- Listening with presence
- Living by the Golden Rule

Preparation isn't just about reading relationship books or listening to sermons—it's about confronting yourself. The real you. The broken you. The unhealed you. And then… choosing better.

The Promise to Prepare

Before anything else, preparation is the key to success

ALEXANDER GRAHAM BELL
Scientist, Engineer, and Inventor of the First Telephone

I made a promise to myself—and to her—that I would not wait until I met her to start becoming who she deserves.

That means reading, studying, learning from wise couples, seeking mentorship, and growing in my character. I don't just want to impress her with who I am. I want to be prepared to serve her, lead her, and grow with her.

Don't romanticize the destination so much that you neglect the preparation.

If you're single, this is the time. Not to pine. Not to chase. But to build. To refine. To shape the man or woman you need to be.

The marriage you long for is not created in the wedding ceremony—it's created in your daily decisions, now.

Secrets of the Successful

Success leaves clues

TONY ROBBINS
World Renowned Life Coach

I once sat across from a couple whose joy was magnetic. I admired their connection. Their ease. Their harmony.

So, I asked them plainly, "How did you build what you have?"

They didn't hesitate. They poured into me—wisdom from years of growth, challenges, victories, and hard-fought unity.

So, here's my advice: Find couples who inspire you. Ask. Learn. Take notes.

People who have great marriages are often eager to share. Not because they think they're perfect—but because they *know* how much work it took.

Let their lessons become your training ground.

Good vs. Great: Which will you Settle for?

Good is an enemy of Great

JIM COLLINS
World renowned best-selling author

Let's define the difference.

A **good marriage** is decent. Respectable. It functions well. There's mutual respect. Some happiness. A solid friendship. They might even raise great kids. It's not bad. But it's not breathtaking either.

A **great marriage?**
That's destiny.
It's two lives fully aligned. Purpose-driven. God-centered. Groundbreaking. Generational.

A great marriage changes more than just two people—it changes entire family trees. It creates wealth. Influence. Impact. Kingdom legacy.

But here's the secret: **Greatness requires intentionality.**

Which one do you want?

Max Jukes and Jonathan Edwards

In the late 1800s, sociologists compared two men and their descendants.

Max Jukes didn't believe in God. He rejected spiritual discipline. He married a woman with similar values.

Of their 1200+ descendants:

- 200 became vagrants
- 130 went to prison
- 100 became alcoholics
- 128 were prostitutes
- Many learned trades in prison
- Total cost to the state: over $1.3 million

Now compare him to **Jonathan Edwards**, a man of deep Christian conviction. He too married a like-minded woman.

Of their descendants:

- 100+ became ministers and missionaries
- 100+ became college professors
- 30 became judges
- 60 became physicians
- 75 served as military officers
- 3 were U.S. Senators
- 1 became Vice President of the United States

What's the difference?

One decision: who they married.

Choose wisely.

In Love with a Person I've Never Met

You're not just picking a spouse. You're setting the course of your lineage.

The Power of Involving Your Family

Don't marry in isolation.
Let your community speak into your decision. Your family. Your mentors. Your spiritual leaders.

If you're hiding the person you're dating from people who love you, ask yourself: *Why?*

The people who have walked with you know your patterns, your calling, and your potential. They can often see what love-blinded eyes cannot.

You're not just building chemistry. You're building covenant. And covenant deserves counsel.

Reject Casual Dating. Pursue Intentional Love.

Every person that is available is not eligible.

UNKNOWN

Casual dating is often a distraction dressed as fun. You spend time. Energy. Emotion. Only to walk away with heartache and regret.

If you desire a love that lasts, treat dating as preparation—not entertainment.

Discipline yourself to wait for what aligns with God's will. Date with purpose. Avoid distractions.

The Promise of Sexual Integrity

The joy of intimacy is the reward of commitment

JOSHUA HARRIS
Author of "I Kissed Dating Goodbye"

There will be moments when loneliness whispers its lies.
Moments when you want companionship so badly it feels like a physical ache.
Moments when it seems easier to compromise than to keep waiting.

But in those moments, remember Joseph.

Tempted. Pursued. Desired.
Yet he said *no*.
Not because he wasn't attracted, but because he was convicted.

And what seemed like a loss in the short term became a promotion in the long term.

Purity protects destiny.
And one moment of restraint can secure a lifetime of joy.

The Storm of Loneliness

Singleness comes in waves.
There are days you love your freedom.
And days you feel the ache of being alone.

It's a storm. But every storm has an end.
Don't let a temporary storm cause you to make a permanent mistake.

The person God has for you is worth the wait.

But more importantly—*you* are worth the wait.
So, treat your heart accordingly.

The Final Promise

You and I must also make the promise to protect.
Not just physically—but emotionally. Spiritually. Verbally.

We must fight to preserve the covenant we make.
Through prayer. Forgiveness. Boundaries. Time.

And above all… we must promise to love until the very end.

The Promise

Dear Future Spouse:

I promise to prepare myself for a wonderful friendship and marriage with you. I will do my best to gain all of the necessary knowledge that it takes in order to become a Great spouse to you and parent for our children. I also promise to preserve my heart for you and no one else. I promise to avoid getting into pointless relationships just for the fun of it because I am willing to sacrifice temporary moments of fun for a lifetime of happiness. I promise to keep my integrity even under pressure. I promise to have faith and not settle for anything less than you. I promise to love you unconditionally despite circumstances and situations. I vow to treasure, love, cherish, and never disrespect the love we share. Honestly, there will be times when it seems that everything in life is perfect. But there will also be moments of sadness, even then I promise to be there for you. I promise to be there for you in sickness and in health. I promise to support you and your dreams. I cannot wait for the opportunity to spend a life growing together. No matter what, I will be standing right beside you, me and my commitment. I will be the best that I can be, I promise!

Scriptural Reflection

"Unless the Lord builds the house, they labor in vain who build it."
—Psalm 127:1 (NKJV)

Let your love be built by the Lord.
Let your heart be framed by His hand.
Let your preparation be a holy offering.
Because when God is the architect, what you build will not only stand…
It will flourish.

CHAPTER

3

When Did Singleness Become a Disease?

Being single doesn't mean you're weak. It means you're strong enough to wait for what you deserve.

NIALL HORAN

It starts like this…

A young woman walks into a doctor's office. Not because she's injured or visibly sick. But because something feels… off. Her body's fine. But her energy is low. Food doesn't taste the same. Work isn't fulfilling. Sleep has become restless. She tells the doctor, "I just feel… incomplete."

He listens, takes notes, and then asks a string of questions that feel oddly personal:

"When was your last date?"
"What's your ideal companion like?"
"How often do you think about love?"
"Do you like romantic movies?"
"Where do you see yourself in ten years?"

He sets down his clipboard, removes his glasses, and says, "Ms. Johnson, I have good news and bad news. The bad news: you've been diagnosed with something called 'singleness.' The good news? It won't kill you."

It's a fictional story—yes. But in our society, doesn't it feel like singleness *has* been pathologized? As though being single is a sign of brokenness, deficiency, or incompleteness?

The unspoken message: If you're single, something must be wrong with you. The reality: If you believe that, something will *become* wrong with you.

So, let me ask the question for all of us:
When did singleness become a disease?

The Stigma of Solitude

There is an invisible but undeniable pressure in our culture to treat singleness as a problem to fix rather than a purpose to fulfill. Our timelines, our dinner conversations, even our churches can sometimes make us feel like relationship status is the measuring stick for maturity.

But let's clear the air: **Singleness is not a disease. It's not a waiting room. It's not a sentence. It's a season—and a sacred one.**

Yes, it can feel uncomfortable at times. Yes, it can be lonely. But so can marriage.
And yet, we've built entire industries—apps, courses, matchmaking services—on the belief that being single is a condition in need of a cure.

It's not.
It's a calling.
And until you embrace that, you'll carry the shame of something God meant to be a gift.

God's View of Singleness

So, what does God actually say about singleness?

In 1 Corinthians 7:32, Paul writes, *"I want you to be free from anxieties. The unmarried man is anxious about the things of the Lord, how to please the Lord."* In other words, singleness is not only acceptable—it is powerful.

It is a space where distractions are fewer, responsibilities are lighter, and focus can be deeper.

God isn't punishing you by keeping you single. He's positioning you. He's inviting you to chase purpose, deepen devotion, expand capacity.

So instead of asking, *"Why am I still single?"* ask, *"What can I build in this season that I couldn't build in any other?"*

Because the truth is, once marriage comes—your time, your energy, your focus will shift. Rightfully so. But if you're single now, this is the moment to lean in.

Singleness is a Season of Personal Growth

The single season is fertile ground for personal growth. This is where emotional maturity is forged, spiritual clarity is developed, and habits that will sustain a marriage are formed.

God has no issue with you desiring companionship. He created that desire. But He also knows that desire, if unchecked by discipline, can become dangerous.

So, what does this mean? It means this is the time to become what you hope to attract.

We often dream about our "ideal" partner. We envision the person who's kind, God-fearing, financially wise, emotionally healthy. But how often do we take a hard look at ourselves and ask, *"Am I becoming that too?"*

Before you're joined to someone else's journey, your single season is the chance to do the deep work of becoming whole.

Stay Single Until…

Stay single until someone adds value to your purpose.
Stay single until their presence brings peace and not pressure.
Stay single until being with them multiplies your joy—not divides your confidence.

Don't just look for someone who looks good in public—look for someone who's healthy in private. Someone who can pray with you when life gets hard. Someone who's healed from their past and not looking for you to fix it.

Be single until someone complements your purpose, not competes with your peace.

Because if the relationship drains your faith, your focus, or your future—it's too expensive.

The "When Are You Getting Married?" Epidemic

Let's talk about it.

If you've been single longer than society expects, you've heard it:

"So, when's the big day?"
"Any prospects?"
"What are you waiting for?"

"You're too cute to be single!"

For the most part, it's harmless small talk. But let's not pretend it doesn't carry weight. Especially when you've been praying. Waiting. Trusting. Hoping.

These questions—though often well-meaning—can pile up into quiet shame. And shame has a funny way of making us settle.

Many people aren't in relationships because they're ready—they're in relationships because they're tired of the questions.

But pressure is not a reason to partner.

When the voices around you become louder than the voice within you, you'll find yourself entertaining what's available instead of waiting for what's aligned.

So how do you respond when people start prying?

Here are a few kind but confident answers:

Q: "When are you getting married?"
A: "Whenever God brings the right one, I'll be ready."

Q: "Any prospects?"
A: "Maybe. But I'm not settling for anything less than purpose."

Q: "Why are you still single?"
A: "Because I value peace over pressure."

When you answer from a place of confidence, people eventually stop asking. But more importantly, *you* stop questioning whether you're behind. You're not.

Singleness is Not a Holding Pattern

There's a myth that life starts when love does.

That you're in "pre-game" until marriage. That you're incomplete until someone picks you.

But let me be clear: You are not a half waiting on a whole.
You are not a résumé waiting on a stamp of approval.
You are not less than.

You are not waiting on life to begin—you're deciding how to build it now.

What you build in your single season will either become a platform for partnership or a prison for pain.

This is the time to build vision. Build habits. Build wealth. Build discipline. Build friendships. Build faith.

Don't wait for someone to join you. Start building. They'll catch up when they're supposed to.

I'd Rather Be Single Than Sorry

Let's be blunt.

A lot of people got married because they were tired of being single.
And now they're married... and tired of being miserable.

They didn't wait. They settled. They ignored red flags. They romanticized potential.

And now, the reality is wearing a name that's hard to escape: regret.

You don't have to end up there.

Waiting well may not be easy, but it's always worth it.
Because when God brings the right one, you won't be guessing. You'll be *grateful*.

So, until then, enjoy your life. Travel. Serve. Grow. Heal.
Be full. Be present. Be joyful.

Because contentment is not found in changing your status.
It's found in changing your perspective.

Don't Perform—Please God

Don't try to please others. Please God.
BISHOP ROBERT LITTLE

We live in a world that performs for likes and applause. But relationships built for Instagram don't last through storms.

You don't have to explain your status to anyone who isn't praying for you.
You don't have to post a person just to prove your worth.
And you don't have to rush into anything to keep people quiet.

God knows the desires of your heart. And He's not just preparing them for you—He's preparing *you* for them.

So, wait well. Live freely. Love deeply.
And most of all, trust God fully.

Because when you trust Him, you don't settle.
You don't strive.

Jeremy Sanford

You don't chase.
You receive.

Scriptural Reflection

"In your patience possess ye your souls."
—Luke 21:19 (KJV)

In a world that wants you to rush, God calls you to *rest*.
In a culture that promotes pressure, God invites you to *patience*.
Your soul is not nourished by speed—it's secured in stillness.

Be still.
Be whole.
Be confident in this: **Your singleness is not a disease.**
It's not a delay.
It's not a mistake.

It's preparation.
It's positioning.
It's a promise in progress.

CHAPTER

4

Single vs. Unmarried

Being single doesn't mean you're weak. It means you're strong enough to wait for what you deserve.

NAILL HORAN

Irish song-writer and guitarist

Let's start with a simple yet thought-provoking question: **Is there a difference between being single and being unmarried?** To many, these terms sound interchangeable. If we surveyed 1,000 people and asked them to differentiate the two, most would likely furrow their brows and say, "Aren't they the same thing?" And on the surface, it would appear so. After all, both terms describe someone who's not married.

But here's the truth—**they are not the same.** In fact, the difference is vast, and the implications are life-altering. When we dig beneath the surface, we uncover two completely different mindsets—two distinct ways of living, thinking, and preparing. One is rooted in purpose and growth. The other is often riddled with confusion, frustration, and delay.

The Unmarried Mindset

Let's begin with the one that many people fall into unknowingly—the unmarried mindset. An **unmarried** person is someone who is not currently in a legal or covenantal marriage. That's a definition most would agree with. But beneath that label lies a troubling reality. Many unmarried individuals walk through life **functionally frustrated, emotionally aimless,** and **spiritually stagnant.** Why? Because they fail to recognize the season they're in. Rather than embracing their current status as a space for preparation, pruning, and personal growth, many spend their time either passively waiting or actively wasting. Their time management is inconsistent. Their spiritual walk is lukewarm. Their emotional boundaries are porous. Their decisions, in many cases, do not reflect the standards or expectations of someone preparing for covenant.

In fact, some unmarried individuals can be found engaging in behaviors that are incompatible with their season—chasing counterfeit relationships, compromising values, or filling their calendars with distractions instead of direction. Over time, these patterns don't just delay purpose—they can derail it.

Let's be clear: **being unmarried doesn't mean someone is ungodly.** But if that person is unaware of how to use their season wisely, it opens the door to disappointment, disillusionment, and sometimes even disobedience.

The Curse of Idle Time

Scripture warns us repeatedly about the dangers of idle time.

> *"Because of laziness the building decays, and through idleness of hands the house leaks."*
> —Ecclesiastes 10:18 (NKJV)

The unmarried person, if unaware, becomes vulnerable to what I call the *curse of idle time*. This isn't some spooky hex—it's the natural consequence of mismanaging a gift that was meant to prepare you for greater.

What's that gift? **Time.**

Time to heal. Time to grow. Time to serve. Time to learn what love looks like in action. Time to become the kind of person you want to marry.

But instead of stewarding this time well, the unmarried person can become trapped in comparison, criticism, and counterfeit connections.

The Single Advantage

Now let's contrast that with the mindset of a **single** person.

When someone truly understands what it means to be single, they don't just tolerate their season—they thrive in it. They are **whole, focused,** and **rooted**. They don't seek a relationship to complete them—they live in the confidence that **only God can do that**.

They recognize that being single is not a waiting room—it's a **workshop**. It's where you prepare, refine, and align with God's purpose for your life.

Single individuals carry themselves with strength. They don't need a title to validate their worth. They don't scroll through social media looking for someone to admire them. Instead, they look in the mirror and say, "I am enough today, and I'm growing into who I need to be for tomorrow."

They aren't desperate for companionship—they're **deliberate with their time, energy, and decisions.**

Let's make it plain:

- The unmarried person says, "Why am I still alone?"
- The single person says, "While I'm here, I'm going to maximize this moment."

Identity vs. Status

Being unmarried is a **status**—something that can change with one ceremony.

Being single, however, is a **state of being**—one that can remain even after someone enters a relationship. Yes, you read that right. You can be married and still not feel whole. You can be in a relationship and still be unsure of your identity. That's because **marriage never heals wounds that weren't first addressed in singleness.**

The single person is secure in their identity. Their joy isn't dependent on a person. Their purpose isn't paused because they don't have a partner. Their spiritual life isn't on hold until they meet "the one."

They are not empty—they are whole. And they know that only two whole people can build a healthy, lasting marriage.

Broken Focus, Broken Expectations

Unmarried individuals often fall into the trap of **chasing relationships rather than cultivating purpose.** They scroll, swipe, text, flirt, compromise—and after all that, they're still empty. Why? Because no relationship can replace preparation. No person can fast-track what only obedience can build.

Many unmarried people are **addicted to the idea of being chosen**, forgetting that they've already been chosen by God.

So, what happens?

They lower their standards. They entertain "almost" love. They justify toxic behaviors. And in doing so, they sabotage the very future they say they want.

The Power of God's Timing

One of the most frustrating things for an unmarried person is **waiting**. Waiting for the right one. Waiting for confirmation. Waiting for love. And often, they believe that the wait means **they're behind**.

But let me encourage you with this:

> *"He has made everything beautiful in its time."*
> —Ecclesiastes 3:11 (NIV)

God's timing is not punishment—it's protection.

What feels like a delay is often divine design. God, in His infinite wisdom, knows when you're ready. He knows what you can handle. He knows when your heart is mature enough to steward the gift of another person. To rush that process is to reject His wisdom.

The single person understands this. They don't just wait—they **prepare while waiting**. They pray, fast, grow, and seek accountability. They ask God, "What are You trying to show me in this season?" rather than begging Him to end it. They don't see singleness as a curse. They see it as **a classroom for character development**.

Becoming Before Belonging

Our culture teaches us to **belong before we become.** It says, "Find someone who loves you, then you'll finally feel like you matter." But kingdom principles flip that: **Become who God called you to be, and in the process, He'll align you with someone who complements—not completes—you.**

The single person embraces this. They wake up daily and ask, "How can I grow today? How can I love better, serve deeper, and hear God more clearly? They understand that if they never become whole, no amount of romance will ever feel like enough.

The Trap of Counterfeits

Unmarried people often fall for counterfeits—not because they're naive, but because they're tired. Tired of waiting. Tired of feeling overlooked. Tired of seeing others "win" at love while they're left questioning their value.

But hear me clearly: **Counterfeits show up when impatience increases.** They look like what you prayed for, but they don't carry the spirit of what God promised. And if you settle for what looks good but isn't God, you'll soon discover that **settling leads to suffering.** The single person isn't fooled by surface. They don't date based on chemistry alone—they look for **character**, **calling**, and **consistency**. They know that it's better to walk alone in alignment than to walk together in dysfunction.

Wholeness Over Romance

Let's be honest—romance feels good. Having someone call you "babe," buy you flowers, or post you on social media can feed the ego.

But wholeness? That feeds the soul.

The single person chooses **soul nourishment over surface attention**. They would rather go without for a season than compromise for a lifetime. They don't chase butterflies—they build gardens.

They understand that marriage is not the prize—**God's purpose is**. And if marriage supports that, great. But if not, they're still fulfilled because their identity isn't rooted in a ring.

Final Thoughts

If you've been living unmarried and frustrated, now is the time to shift into **singleness and freedom**.

Not because someone's coming soon—but because God has something for you **now**. There's purpose in this season. There's power in your preparation. And there's beauty in becoming the best version of yourself.

Don't just count the days until you meet someone—**make the days count**. Become. Grow. Lead. Heal. Serve. Worship. And when the right person comes, they'll meet someone who's not desperate for love—but filled with it.

Scriptural Reflection

> *"For your Maker is your husband—the Lord Almighty is his name—the Holy One of Israel is your Redeemer; he is called the God of all the earth."*
> —Isaiah 54:5 (NIV)

This verse serves as a holy reminder that **our first covenant is with God**. Before you are ever joined with another, you are already deeply known, fiercely loved, and eternally claimed by your Creator.

Jeremy Sanford

The season of singleness is not a placeholder—it's a **partnership with heaven**. You are not waiting to be chosen. You already are. You're not lacking love. You walk in it. And you're not alone—He is with you.

So, take heart. Embrace the beauty of being single—not as an absence, but as an assignment.

Because when you walk with God, you never walk alone.

CHAPTER

5

Maximizing Your Potential

*Hope for love, pray for love, wish for love, dream for love...
but don't put your life on hold waiting for Love.*

MANDY HALE
Christian Author & Blogger

Love is eternal, yet the seasons we walk through are not. Love transcends time, but seasons—whether marked by joy or sorrow—are temporary. They come. They go. But each one has a purpose. In life, just as in nature, seasons are signposts. They shape our stories. They become the backdrop for our memories, the milestones of our growth. When people reflect on their lives, they often recount the seasons that defined them: seasons of childhood, of discovery, of success, of heartbreak.

But here's the truth we often miss: seasons are not just about time—they're about transformation.

One season, one moment, one decision can change everything.

How you show up in your current season can anchor you in destiny or detour you into regret. The choice is yours.

The Power of a Single Decision

Any parent understands this instinctively. That's why they constantly say things like, "Choose your friends wisely," or "Respect your teachers," or "Stay focused." They're not nagging. They're investing. They're planting seeds of wisdom because they know one decision can shift the trajectory of a life.

Picture John, an 8-year-old boy growing up with loving parents who model integrity. Though not wealthy, his parents offer him something more valuable: vision, values, and belief in his potential. But as John enters adolescence, the atmosphere around him shifts. The streets whisper temptations. Gangs and peer pressure tighten their grip. It starts with small compromises—a skipped homework assignment here, a defiant comment to a teacher there. The slide is subtle, but swift.

By the time John reaches high school, he's no longer drifting—he's sinking. His parents still love him deeply. But the world won't see the values he was raised with; they'll only judge the season where he stumbled.

That's the weight of one season. One choice. One compromise. It can cost everything.

Singleness: A Sacred Season

You might be asking, "What does this have to do with being single?"

Everything.

Because how you navigate your season of singleness determines what you carry into your next season. And make no mistake—this season matters.

Singleness is not a time to pause your life. It's a time to prepare for it.

It's not a void to be filled. It's a canvas to be painted. It's not a waiting room. It's a workshop.

Investing in the Right Season

Let's flip the narrative.

Instead of someone who missed their moment, let's highlight someone who maximized theirs: Steve Jobs.

In his early 20s, while many of his peers were killing time, Jobs was building Apple. His intense focus, curiosity, and refusal to waste time created one of the most iconic companies in history. He wasn't waiting for life to begin—he was shaping it.

That's what happens when you steward your season.

So, if you're single right now, don't despise this time. Embrace it. Steward it.

I'm walking with you. I'm your partner in this. Your motivator. Your coach.

Call Me Coach

I absolutely believe that people, unless coached, never reach their maximum capabilities.

BOB NARDELLI
Former CEO of Home Depot & Chrysler

In every sport, elite athletes don't rise to the top by chance. They train. They refine. They have vision. But most of all, they have coaches.

A coach sees what you can't. A coach stretches you, challenges you, corrects you, and calls out the greatness buried under insecurity and fear.

If you want a healthy marriage, a meaningful life, a legacy that outlives you—then start with this question: who are you becoming?

You don't attract what you want. You attract who you are.

Ladies, if you're praying for a man of faith, character, and consistency, then your focus should be on becoming a woman of grace, depth, and discipline.

Gentlemen, don't just desire a Proverbs 31 woman—become a man worthy of her trust, her respect, and her "yes."

Self-development isn't selfish. It's spiritual stewardship.

Frustrated or Focused?

There are only two ways to navigate your single season: frustrated or focused.

Frustrated singleness is like driving with one foot on the gas and the other on the brake. You move, but never with momentum. You're exhausted, but not advancing.

It leads to:

- Desperate dating
- Unnecessary heartbreak
- Cycles of emotional confusion
- Relationships that subtract more than they add

But focused singleness? That's where the magic happens.

Focused singles are intentional. They treat this season as preparation, not punishment.

They write vision. They travel. They launch businesses. They study the Word. They go to therapy. They learn to love their own company.

They grow emotionally, spiritually, financially. They evolve.

And as they do, they become magnets. Not for everyone. But for the right one.

Building, Not Just Budgeting

Let's pause and talk about money.

Most singles don't realize the financial gift this season offers. Without the responsibilities of a spouse or children, you have unparalleled freedom.

This is the time to build.

Build savings. Build discipline. Build investment knowledge. Build habits that will serve you in every season of life.

Even if you're not earning six figures, you can master stewardship. Start by:

- Creating a budget
- Eliminating debt
- Saving consistently
- Investing wisely

Your future marriage doesn't need a fairy tale—it needs a foundation.

Don't just bring love into the relationship. Bring stability. Bring vision. Bring strategy.

Your single years are not just about preparing your heart. They're about preparing your house.

Discover the Hidden Gifts of Singleness

God doesn't waste time, pain, or seasons.

Singleness is not a penalty. It's a divine opportunity.

It comes with gifts—hidden treasures disguised as freedom, flexibility, and clarity.

Here's what you can unwrap:

- **Clarity of Calling**: With fewer distractions, you can hear God's voice more clearly.
- **Freedom to Serve**: You have mobility. You can go where God sends without negotiation.
- **Deep Friendships**: This is the time to cultivate rich, platonic relationships that ground and grow you.
- **Spiritual Intimacy**: You have time to go deep with God. No competing demands. Just communion.

These are not consolation prizes. These are kingdom tools.

Singleness is not second-class. It is sacred ground.

The Promise of Becoming

At its core, this season is not about doing. It's about becoming.

You are not incomplete. You are not on hold. You are a whole person being refined, shaped, and strengthened.

Marriage is not your finish line. It's your next assignment.

And the best way to honor that future is to embrace this season of becoming.

Become joyful now.

Become wise now.

Become faithful now.

Become disciplined now.

Because when the next season arrives, you won't be scrambling to catch up—you'll be prepared to thrive.

Scripture Reflection: The Power of Preparation

> *"To everything there is a season, and a time to every purpose under the heaven."*
> —Ecclesiastes 3:1 (KJV)

This verse is a divine reminder: seasons are not random. They are divinely orchestrated.

The God who hung the stars also set your timeline. And He wastes nothing.

David was anointed king long before he wore a crown. Those in-between years were not wasted—they were essential. He fought battles, wrote Psalms, learned leadership. He became before he reigned.

Even Jesus honored the process. He spent 30 years in preparation for 3 years of ministry. If the Son of God needed a season of growth, so do we.

So don't resent your singleness. Redeem it.

Ask God:

- What are You cultivating in me?
- What kind of character are You forming?
- What can I sow now that will bless my next chapter?

You are not just waiting for the one.

You are becoming the one.

Maximize this season. Steward it well. The future you're praying for depends on the choices you make today.

CHAPTER

6

My Singleness Has an Expiration Date

*Hope for love, pray for love, wish for love, dream for love...
but don't put your life on hold waiting for Love*

MANDY HALE
Christian Author & Blogger

Everybody Has Somebody Except Me

Some mornings just hit differently. You wake up, take a deep breath, and before your feet even touch the ground, it's like your *environment* decided to whisper one subtle but unrelenting message: *Everybody has somebody—except you.*

This was one of those mornings.

As I stepped out of my front door, the crisp air wrapped around me, and I could almost smell it—love. It was in the breeze, in the silence between chirping birds, and it seemed to be stitched into the very fabric of the day.

I hopped into my car, ready to face whatever tasks the day would bring, but it felt like love was being showcased at every corner.

At the first red light, I noticed them—my retired neighbors. Grey-haired, slow-paced, fingers laced together, walking the sidewalk as if the years had only deepened their affection. She tossed her head back in laughter while he said something I couldn't hear but could feel. It was love—simple, seasoned, enduring.

Next, I hit a school zone. Children rushed across crosswalks, backpacks bouncing and sneakers squeaking. Right in the middle of the chaos, a family caught my eye. Two parents, one boy, one girl—morning routines in motion. The mother gently tucked the little girl's hair behind her ear. The father leaned down to tie his son's shoe. Kisses were exchanged, bags adjusted, and off the kids went into their day. Another reminder—everybody has somebody.

The pattern continued.

Elevator rides with colleagues sweet-talking their partners. Office visits where desks were adorned with smiling family portraits, vacation snapshots, and wedding-day memories. Even a walk through the park during my lunch break turned into a montage of affection—hand-holding couples, young kids playfully exchanging flowers, and romantic energy dancing on the edges of every interaction.

By the time I saw the stunning young woman drop her sunglasses and I rushed to return them—only for her boyfriend to swoop in and claim her company—I'd reached my limit.

Seriously? I thought. *Does love just orbit around everyone but me?*

When Love Seems to Be Everywhere but with You

Let's be honest: some days make your singleness feel more like a sentence than a season. The sky seems bluer for couples. Coffee shops feel louder with laughter that's not yours. Instagram scrolls feel like emotional warfare. And even five-year-olds with daisies remind you that companionship is everywhere—but not in your arms.

And what makes it worse is that you know you're a catch. You're educated, driven, God-fearing, and emotionally available. You've got values. You've got vision. You've even healed from your past (mostly). So why does it feel like love is playing a cruel game of hide and seek—only without the seeking?

This isn't just frustration. It's *weariness*. It's not that you don't believe love will come—it's the exhausting wondering about *when*, *how*, and *why not yet*.

But what if I told you—you're not the first to feel this way?

You're Not the First

Writers are the main landmarks of the past.
EDWARD BULWER-LYTTON

The idea that *everybody has somebody except me* is older than hashtags, Hallmark cards, and Tinder profiles. In fact, it's as old as humanity itself.

Consider Adam—the very first man created by God.

In the Book of Genesis, Adam is given a monumental assignment: to name every animal on the planet. One by one, the creatures come. The elephant with its wrinkled trunk. The giraffe with its regal neck. The lion with its kingly roar. And as Adam fulfills this divine task, he notices something peculiar: every animal has a companion.

Every *kind* had a counterpart. Every species was formed in pairs.

Except him.

And suddenly, it hits him.

Everyone has somebody—except me.

God, in His infinite wisdom, didn't rebuke Adam's longing. He didn't shame his desire for connection. Instead, He responded by saying, *"It is not good for man to be alone"* (Genesis 2:18). And from Adam's side, God formed Eve—the one who was not only helpful but also suitable. A partner. A friend. A companion designed not just for functionality, but for *fit*.

That's the kind of love worth waiting for—not just a person who's helpful, but someone who's divinely suitable.

Helped and Suitable

Too often, we settle for people who are simply *helpful*. They look good on paper. They're kind. They check a few boxes. But they're not *suitable*. Their values don't align. Their purpose doesn't match. **The rhythm of your purpose doesn't dance to their life song.**

That's why it's not just about having someone—it's about having the *right* someone.

Eve wasn't just Adam's match biologically. She was his match *destiny-wise*. She shared his space, his mission, his rhythm.

So yes, it's okay to want someone. It's even okay to ache for connection on those long, love-filled days. But never let your longing lead you to settle for a help that isn't suitable.

Use Your Isolation as a Landmark

These days—when it feels like everyone is in love except you—aren't wasted. In fact, they are sacred.

Mark them.

Journal them.

Record what you feel. Because one day, when love does arrive, you'll look back on this season and say, "I remember when I felt forgotten." And that memory will deepen your gratitude.

It will also deepen your compassion.

Don't be the person who finds love and then forgets the pain of waiting. Let your journey become an encouraging word for someone else's delay. Use your story as a testimony, not just a memory.

Jesus once said, *"The poor you will always have with you."* In the same way, there will always be those who are single, longing, waiting. You're not just called to *receive* love—you're called to *reflect* it, even in how you encourage others in their season.

Faith in the Waiting

Waiting is not weakness. It's often the training ground of faith.

God is not punishing you. He is *preparing* you.

It may feel like everyone else got their delivery—like Amazon Prime skipped your house—but God's delivery system is unlike ours. He gives no tracking number. No ETA. But He gives a confirmation: His Word.

The Bible says, *"Faith is the substance of things hoped for, the evidence of things not seen."* (Hebrews 11:1)

Faith doesn't always give you proof—but it does give you peace.

Your relationship, your spouse, your "somebody" is not lost. It's just scheduled for an arrival that you don't control. So instead of trying to rush the process, rest in the promise.

Can You Hear Him?

The Bible is the Word of God in such a way that when the Bible speaks, God speaks.

B.B. WARFIELD

Many of us pray daily—sometimes even desperately—asking God to speak. "Lord, show me if he's the one." "God, is she my wife?" "Why haven't You brought me someone yet?"

And then we leave our prayer closet frustrated, convinced that God is silent.

But God's not silent. We're just not always listening.

God speaks most clearly through His Word. His promises. His principles. If your prayer life is rich but your Word life is weak, don't be surprised when you feel directionless. His answers are often in the pages we ignore.

So next time you feel alone, open your Bible and hear Him again.

In Love with a Person I've Never Met

Qualified Advice Only

Let's clear something up. Everybody has an opinion about relationships. But not everyone is *qualified* to give you advice.

Some people mean well—but they're on marriage number three. Others give strong opinions but are bitter, broken, or living vicariously through your love life.

Be wise. If someone hasn't succeeded in the area you're pursuing, receive their input with caution. Listen to people whose relationships reflect what you desire—not just people who *talk* a good game.

As the saying goes, "Don't take financial advice from broke people. Don't take relationship advice from bitter ones."

Good Things Take Time

"If anyone would come after me, let him deny himself..."
—Matthew 16:24 (ESV)

Jesus taught us that following Him requires self-denial—a principle often overlooked in a generation obsessed with immediacy.

Sometimes God delays a relationship not because you're unworthy—but because He's protecting you from premature connection.

Impatience leads to Ishmael. But patience positions you for Isaac.

God hasn't forgotten you. He's fashioning someone who doesn't just meet your eyes but meets your spirit. Don't settle for what's available—wait for what's *appointed*.

Scriptural Reflection

"We have this hope as an anchor for the soul, firm and secure."
—Hebrews 6:19 (NIV)

Hope is not a soft feeling—it's a soul anchor.

On the days when loneliness whispers, when comparison shouts, when the ache becomes unbearable—hope steadies you.

When you believe God's Word over your feelings, your soul finds rest, even when love hasn't yet arrived.

You are not forgotten. You are not invisible. You are not late.

God's timeline is perfect. And when the appointed time comes, you'll see why the wait was worth it.

Until then, live fully. Love freely. Trust deeply. And anchor your soul in hope.

CHAPTER

7

The License to Hunt

*To hunt successfully, you must know your ground,
your pack, and your quarry.*

TIM HOLT
Award winning British novelist

The License to Hunt

Let's be honest. If you skipped ahead to this chapter, you're not alone.

For many, the idea of pursuing love—or being pursued—is the most compelling topic in the book. Whether you're male or female, young or seasoned, odds are you've imagined how the moment might come: the conversation, the chemistry, the chase. You've thought about love, maybe longed for it, and certainly hoped for the real thing.

But here's the truth many won't say out loud: **most people want love but have no idea how to pursue it—or prepare for it**. They want the reward without the risk. The romance without the rejection. The commitment without the courage.

In real hunting, nobody just grabs a shotgun, runs into the woods, and shoots at anything that moves. There's preparation involved. Study. Practice.

Strategy. **And most importantly—there's a license.** You don't hunt unless you're authorized and equipped to do so.

The same is true in love. Before you go after "the one," you need clarity, courage, and character. But before we hand you that symbolic license to pursue a relationship, we have to deal with the one thing stopping most people from experiencing the love they desire:

Fear.

Beyond Fear

Everything you want is on the other side of fear.

DR. FARRAH GRAY

Fear is the most paralyzing force when it comes to relationships. It's silent but powerful. And it wears different faces for different people.

For many **men**, it's the fear of rejection. The anxiety of hearing "no." The fear that approaching someone could bruise their confidence or dignity.

For **women**, it's the fear of loneliness. That silent whisper that says, "What if I end up alone?" Or worse: "What if I have to settle?"

Both fears are valid—but neither should have authority over your future.

Here's what we must understand: **Fear is the enemy of faith.** The two cannot coexist. Hebrews 11:6 reminds us that without faith, it is impossible to please God. That doesn't just apply to salvation or finances—it applies to relationships too.

Fear distorts perception. It exaggerates worst-case scenarios. It makes walking across a room to say hello feel like crossing a battlefield.

Let me be real—especially to the men reading this.

You're not dodging bullets. You're not in a war zone. Walking up to say hello will not result in physical harm or emotional dismemberment. The worst that can happen is a polite "no."

That's it.

If the woman you approach isn't interested, life goes on. But if you never try, you'll live with the torment of "what if?" And trust me—**regret weighs more than rejection.**

The Art of Resilience

Let me share a quick story.

I once saw a woman at a national church conference that caught my attention immediately. She had the kind of style that turns heads without trying—graceful, intelligent, elegant. Long hair. Designer glasses. The kind of woman who probably knew **the periodic table of elements by heart**, yet also had a Pinterest board full of fashion.

I spotted her browsing books. I checked—no boyfriend nearby, no ring on her finger. After hyping myself up, I walked over and said the first thing I could think of: "Do you know where they're selling the DVDs from the service?"

Corny? Sure. But it got us talking.

After she kindly gave me directions, I went downstairs for a few minutes, then circled back to thank her. We talked briefly. She was from New York, had a master's degree, and exuded confidence.

Then came the moment of truth.

"Would it be okay if we kept in touch?"

She smiled politely. "You seem very nice, but I'd rather not."

Now pause right there.

Was I crushed? Momentarily.

But did it define me? Absolutely not.

The next day, I met someone else equally engaging, and this time, the connection clicked.

That's what resilience looks like. The ability to shake off disappointment and move forward without bitterness or self-hate.

Too often, we internalize rejection:

- "Maybe I'm not attractive enough."
- "Maybe I'm too awkward."
- "Maybe I'm just not enough."

But sometimes, the "no" has nothing to do with you. I later learned she was already in a relationship. I didn't know that at the time, but it confirmed an important truth:

Stop blaming yourself for someone else's unknown context.

Rejection Isn't Fatal

Men, hear me: the key to successful pursuit is confidence—not arrogance, but quiet assurance that you are valuable. That you bring something to the table. That if one person can't see that, someone else will.

The only thing worse than hearing "no" is never giving yourself a chance to hear "yes."

Fear keeps you paralyzed.

Regret keeps you haunted.

But faith? Faith keeps you moving.

Ladies: Release the Fear of Being Alone

Now, ladies—let's talk.

The fear of being alone is one of the most dangerous emotional traps. It creates an invisible tension that repels the very thing you want to attract. A woman driven by the fear of loneliness radiates anxiety—and whether you realize it or not, **men can sense that energy.**

Desperation, even if well-disguised, always leaves a scent.

And men—especially high-value, intentional men—can smell it from a mile away.

So how do you avoid this?

By shifting your focus from **desire** to **development**.

Focus on becoming happy, healthy, and whole—right now. The more joy you generate within, the more magnetic your presence becomes. Be confident. Be grateful. Be generous. Gratitude transforms your atmosphere. Positivity makes you radiant.

Want to make yourself irresistible?

Be so full of life that any man who joins you sees it as a privilege—not a rescue mission.

Understand Your Prey

This might sound primitive, but it's necessary: to engage in the pursuit of love, you must understand the species.

Men are **visual**. They are drawn to what they see—before they process what they feel. That's not shallowness; it's design.

So yes, **how you present yourself matters.**

That doesn't mean looking like a supermodel every day. It means putting care and intentionality into how you show up—how you dress, how you carry yourself, how you treat others. Because believe it or not, men often "date from a distance." They watch. They observe. They gather information long before they ever say hello.

Your character speaks even when your lips don't.

And when the right man is watching, you want your life, your energy, your faith, and your presence to tell the truth: **"I'm ready."**

Different Hunters, Different Targets

Not all men are hunting the same thing. Some are looking for beauty. Some are looking for security. Some are looking for depth. And a few? A few are looking for a destiny partner—someone who doesn't just match their moment but amplifies their mission.

So, here's your job—**know what kind of "hunter" you want to attract.**

Men, write it down: What kind of woman are you truly looking for?

Ladies, make your list too. Then write a second list: Who do I need to become to attract that kind of partner?

At the bottom of that list, write this bold declaration:
"**I trust God.**"

Because even with all the insight, preparation, and strategy—**only God can orchestrate divine alignment.**

Getting My Rib Back

No single man will ever be complete until he gets his rib back.

BISHOP JOHN T. LESLIE

From the beginning, man was created with a void—a missing rib. And from that rib, woman was formed. Embedded in that story is a powerful truth: **men were made to pursue what completes them.**

So, ladies, rest assured: you're not being overlooked. Someone is looking for you. Someone is preparing to pursue you. And if you posture yourself correctly, you won't have to chase love—**you'll attract it.**

At the same time, men must know this: we don't just need beauty. We need substance. Kindness. Compassion. Discipline. Peace. Purpose. The kind of qualities that endure beyond attraction and into legacy.

Marriage is not a sprint. It's a marathon. And only marriage covenants built on character will survive the storms.

Final Thoughts: The Pursuit That Leads to Peace

You don't marry someone you can live with.
You marry someone you can't imagine living without.

Pursue wisely. Choose intentionally. And don't settle.

Because when love is right—really right—you won't have to force it. You'll just find yourself smiling more, praying deeper, and thanking God that fear didn't keep you from trying.

Now that you've gained insight…

You officially have your **License to Hunt.**

Scriptural Reflection

"For God has not given us a spirit of fear, but of power and of love and of a sound mind."
—2 Timothy 1:7 (NKJV)

This is your spiritual license. Your divine release from fear. The next time your heart races at the thought of approaching someone—or believing God for something you haven't yet seen—remember this verse. You were not created to shrink. You were created to pursue with boldness, built in wisdom, and covered in grace.

Go forward. Fearlessly.

CHAPTER

8

Attraction Psychology

The law of attraction is this: You don't attract what you want. You attract what you are.

DR. WAYNE DYER
Internationally renowned author and speaker in the field of self-development

Let's be honest—we can talk about spiritual matters all day, but when it comes to attraction, we live in a real world where principles matter. I would be remiss if I wrote an entire book on singleness without addressing the elements that make a person attractive to the opposite sex. Yes, faith is crucial. But knowledge? It gives your faith hands and feet.

Faith is the substance of things hoped for, the evidence of things not seen (Hebrews 11:1). But Hosea 4:6 warns us that "My people are destroyed for lack of knowledge." That means faith without knowledge is like trying to build a house with no blueprint. You can believe all you want that your dream home will appear, but if you never lay a foundation or hammer a nail, all you'll ever have is the hope.

Right now, I have faith that I will marry an incredible woman—driven, beautiful, full of life. But if I don't have the knowledge to know how to meet, attract, or connect with her, my faith may never translate into reality. Knowledge increases capacity. It expands your ability to act on your faith.

This is true whether you're building a business, launching a dream, or finding a life partner.

Now, full transparency—I recently met a woman who checks a lot of those boxes. She's educated, beautiful, and full of adventure. Could she be the one? Maybe. You'll have to keep reading to find out.

As a single person, I've attended more singles conferences than I can count. Many focus on self-improvement and waiting on God. While valuable, I often leave with questions like:

- What do I do when I see someone I'm attracted to?
- How do I spark a meaningful conversation?
- What exactly are men and women looking for today?

These are the real-world issues singles face. That's why this book dives deeper than platitudes. Christians need practical strategies too. We need to understand not just what to pray for, but how to prepare, pursue, and position ourselves.

How to get a Woman

Often the thing we fear the most is the thing we want the most.

DR. MATT JONES
3-Time cancer survivor and motivational speaker

Let's get one thing straight: approaching a woman you're attracted to can feel like walking a tightrope with no net. But it doesn't have to be that way. Let me share a few practical tips:

1. **Move quickly.** Use the three-second rule. The moment you spot her, scan for a ring or nearby male companion. If she's not married and

not occupied, go. Don't overthink. The longer you delay, the more your nerves will talk you out of it.

2. **Be honest.** Ditch the pickup lines. Say something like, "Hi, I saw you across the room and wanted to introduce myself." Women appreciate sincerity. It communicates confidence and maturity.
3. **Compliment her.** Sincerely point out something you noticed—her smile, outfit, or presence. Keep it classy.
4. **Ask thoughtful questions.** Don't just fire off queries. Show interest. Be curious about her thoughts, goals, or passions.
5. **Smile and nod.** Active listening speaks volumes. It shows that you value what she's saying.
6. **Get the number.** When the energy feels right, say, "It was great talking to you. Put your number in my phone so we can continue this later." Hand her the phone. Confidence breeds results.
7. **Exit gracefully.** Leave on a high note. Don't linger. You've created anticipation. Let it breathe.
8. **Follow up.** Don't wait forever. Two days max. Any longer suggests disinterest.

Dress for Success

You can have anything you want. If you dress for it.

EDITH HEAD

American costume designer, won eight Academy Awards for Best Costume design

Let's be real—visuals matter. You don't have to be a model, but you should take pride in your appearance. Dress like someone who values themselves. Want to catch the attention of a high-quality partner? Then look like you're headed somewhere in life.

That applies in church, too. If you're believing God for a virtuous spouse, show up looking like you believe for that level of favor. And don't just dress for where you are—dress for where you're going. Aspire to CEO status? Look the part now.

But more than clothes, chase after God. A godly man is drawn to a woman who radiates purpose and presence. And ladies, the same goes for you. The most attractive person in the room is often the one most in tune with their divine assignment.

How to Attract a Man

A busy, vibrant, goal-oriented woman is much more attractive than one who waits for a man to validate her existence.

MANDY HALE
Christian Author & Blogger

Men are drawn to women who know who they are. Women who have passion, direction, and purpose. Don't wait to build a life around a man—build it now. That way, the right man won't be your source of identity, he'll be a partner in destiny.

When a woman has goals, it's magnetic. Are you starting a business? Writing a book? Leading in your community? That's attractive.

When the right man comes, share your passions. Let him know what you bring to the table. Don't shrink. Shine.

And yes—your appearance matters too. Men are visual creatures. That doesn't mean you have to fit a mold, but be intentional. Own your femininity. Show up polished and poised.

Don't Be Negative

*Some people are so negative that they could
go into a dark room and develop.*

DR. FARRAH GRAY

Negativity is a dealbreaker. Men want a woman they can laugh with, dream with, and exhale with. Show your fun side. Be joyful. Let your personality shine.

Proverbs 21:9 says, "It is better to dwell in the corner of a housetop than with a brawling woman in a wide house." Don't be a source of stress. Be a source of peace.

Encouragement is powerful. Be the kind of woman that builds a man up with your words. When he talks about his goals, cheer him on. Offer insight. Speak life.

Confidence is key. A confident woman knows her worth and doesn't settle. She walks in rooms like she belongs there—because she does. She's the kind of woman who gets introduced to Mom. Trust me—not every woman gets to meet Mom.

Traits Men Love

Find someone that celebrates you and not just tolerates you.

JARRET PERDUE
Pentecostal Assemblies of the World International Youth President

Ladies, when you finally do run into the man of your dreams, be ready to lift him up and be a support system in the midst a society that bombards us with negativity each day.

- **Independence:** Show him you have a full life. Hobbies, goals, relationships. Men want to join your world, not become your world.
- **Strength:** Life isn't easy. Can you stand through storms? Men want a woman who can endure, pray, and believe with them.
- **Vulnerability:** Strength doesn't mean hiding your heart. Show your softness. Be real about your needs. Let him feel needed.
- **Femininity:** Be a woman, fully. Embrace your softness, your style, your nurturing nature. It's not weakness—it's power.
- **Happiness:** Joy is magnetic. Smile. Laugh. Enjoy your life. A happy woman draws people to her like light in a dark room.

Ladies, a man doesn't want a perfect woman. He wants a woman who knows her value, walks in her purpose, and lights up the world around her. When you're that kind of woman, he will recognize it—and if he doesn't, you haven't lost anything. You've just made room for someone better.

Gentlemen, the same applies to you. Dress well, walk in purpose, pursue with confidence, and be honest. When your character matches your calling, the woman of your dreams won't be far away.

Before we close this chapter, let me give you a preview of what's next. In the upcoming chapter, we'll dive into the power of **visualizing your soul mate**—because once you begin to attract the right kind of attention (and you will), you'll need clarity to discern who truly aligns with your purpose. Attraction alone isn't enough; it's vision that helps you recognize covenant potential when it stands in front of you.

Oh—and remember that intriguing young lady I mentioned earlier? The one I recently met who seems to check all the right boxes? She's still in the picture. Beautiful. Educated. Adventurous. Could she be the one? Maybe. Maybe not. You'll have to keep reading to find out.

Scriptural Reflection

*"Delight yourself in the LORD, and He will
give you the desires of your heart."*

—Psalm 37:4 (ESV)

This verse isn't about getting whatever we want. It's about aligning our desires with God's purpose. When your life is focused on God, you begin to attract what complements your calling.

Attraction isn't about manipulation. It's about magnetism. Become the person you want to attract. Let God refine your character. Let wisdom inform your actions. And when the time is right, you won't have to chase love—it will find you walking in purpose.

CHAPTER

9

The Power of Visualization

Losers visualize the penalties of failure. Winners visualize the rewards of success.

WILLIAM S. GILBERT
English physician, physicist, and natural philosopher

Forgive me for leaving you on a cliffhanger in the last chapter—I didn't mean to stir up suspense without a proper resolution. But as promised, let me tell you more about the intriguing young lady I recently met.

I serve as a youth leader at my church, a role I love deeply. Every Friday night, we host youth services packed with energy, purpose, and spiritual enrichment. My team and I often implement monthly themed services to keep things dynamic and engaging. One such service brought together guests from across the country. That night, amidst the vibrant gathering, I saw her.

We had never officially met, but thanks to social media and mutual connections, she wasn't a stranger to me. When the time came to greet visitors, I made my way over and introduced myself. She was petite, poised, and clearly comfortable in the room. She didn't carry herself like a guest—she felt like family. My peers loved her energy. She blended seamlessly with the group, and I found myself drawn in.

As the weekend progressed, we talked more. On her last day in town, we had breakfast together. I discovered she was driven, educated, and had a zest for life. It sparked something in me—curiosity, maybe even hope. After she left, I couldn't help but think, "She might be worth exploring further."

We followed up with a phone conversation a few days later. Our lives are busy—mine with ministry and work, hers with school and career. The conversation flowed, but if I'm honest, something felt unclear. I was interested. She seemed... maybe. Sometimes the spark is mutual and undeniable. This time? It wasn't. Was she playing it cool? Or was I reading too much into a moment?

I won't say she's not the one, but I'm not going to stress it either. I'll see her at an event soon, and maybe we'll reconnect. Until then, I'm focused forward.

Enough about me—let's talk visualization.

Visualization is one of the most powerful tools for success. Whether it's athletics, business, relationships, or faith, the ability to see the future before it arrives is the secret sauce for greatness. Visualization is painting your future on the canvas of your imagination. It allows you to move with confidence, clarity, and certainty.

Arnold Schwarzenegger is a perfect example. As a young bodybuilder, he visualized becoming like his idol Reg Park. He said, "The model was there in my mind; I only had to grow enough to fill it." Schwarzenegger didn't stop with fitness—he used visualization in acting and politics. "Create a vision of who you want to be and then live that picture as if it is already true."

Olympic gold medalist Lindsey Vonn visualized her ski runs hundreds of times in her mind before competing. She saw the course, the turns, the breathing patterns. When race time came, her body simply followed the script her mind had rehearsed.

Visualize Better

If you can see it and believe it, it is a lot easier to achieve it.

OPRAH WINFREY
Talk show host, actress, producer, and philanthropist

Even as a child, Oprah used visualization. Watching her grandmother work tirelessly, she would say to herself, "My life won't be like this. It will be better." That inner image of a different future drove her to become one of the most influential women in history.

Visualize Greatness

He who says he can and he who says he can't are both usually right

CONFUCIUS
Influential Chinese philosopher

Will Smith once said, "In my mind, I've always been an A-list Hollywood superstar. Y'all just didn't know yet." He saw the version of himself the world had yet to see, and he acted like it until it became real.

So how do you practice visualization?

Start with 15 minutes. Find a quiet place. See your future with clarity. Think about your spouse, your purpose, your calling. What kind of marriage do you want? What kind of person will you be?

Then pray. Acknowledge God in your dreams. Align your vision with His will. If you don't hear from Him right away, don't worry. Keep praying. Keep seeking. The right direction will emerge over time.

Faith Therapy

I would visualize things coming to me. It would make me feel better. Visualization works if you work hard.

JIM CARREY

Visualization is not just dreaming—it's therapy. It calms your fears, restores your hope, and gives clarity to your path. When you visualize your future, you start living with intentionality.

Even when life disappoints—when friends betray you, promotions pass you, or relationships fizzle out—visualization reminds you that your destiny is still intact. You are not defined by detours.

Colonel Sanders was rejected over 300 times before someone believed in his fried chicken recipe. Jack Canfield faced 30+ rejections for *Chicken Soup for the Soul*. But their belief in a better future kept them pressing forward. And they changed the world.

So, let's get practical. Read this aloud, then close your eyes and imagine it:

> "I am currently in a wonderful and loving marriage. My marriage is a beautiful union put together by God..."

Now, create your own vision. Adjust your visualization based on the life you want. Better yet, build a vision board. Print images that reflect your dreams—your marriage, career, family, spiritual life. Place them where you can see them daily. Remind yourself of where you're going.

Develop Your Faith

"Now faith is the substance of things hoped for, the evidence of things not seen."
—Hebrews 11:1

Faith and visualization walk hand in hand. Where the world calls it manifestation, we as believers call it trust in God. But trust alone is not enough—you must act. James 2:26 reminds us that "faith without works is dead."

Ladies, if you want your future husband to sweep you off your feet, let your lifestyle align with your vision. Prepare for the kind of love you want.

Gentlemen, don't just wish for a great wife—go after her. The Bible says, "He who finds a wife finds a good thing." You have to seek. Pursue. Move with confidence. Don't be lazy.

Faith Confidence

With confidence you have won before you have started.
MARCUS GARVEY

Your body language often speaks before your mouth ever opens. Faith can be seen. When you believe your dreams are coming, you walk differently. Your shoulders are square. Your eyes are lifted. Your steps are sure.

If you're walking around discouraged, defeated, and desperate, it's time to check your faith. When you believe God is working behind the scenes, you don't panic. You prepare.

See your future. Speak it. Step into it. And don't let doubt rob you of what God already planned.

Before we wrap this up, remember what we said at the end of the last chapter. Once you begin to attract people (and you will), you need to know how to filter. That's where visualization comes in. See the kind of love you want—not just in theory, but in detail. So when it shows up, you'll recognize it.

Oh—and yes, I'll keep you posted on the young lady I mentioned earlier. Our story isn't over yet. Maybe she's the one. Maybe she's not. Time will tell.

Scriptural Reflection

> *"Write the vision, and make it plain upon tables, that he may run that readeth it."*
>
> —Habakkuk 2:2 (KJV)

God doesn't just want you to dream—He wants you to define the dream. Write it down. Visualize it. Pray over it. Run with it. When you align your vision with heaven, the future becomes more than a hope—it becomes a calling.

So start seeing it. Speak it. And don't stop believing until it becomes your reality.

CHAPTER

10

The List

The indispensable first step to getting the things you want out of life is this: decide what you want.

BEN STEIN
Actor and author

Let's be honest: single people usually carry a mental—or physical—list of what they want in a spouse. Whether tucked away in a drawer or embedded in memory, the "list" exists. It's the description of our ideal match—our must-haves, our non-negotiables, our dreams for what love should look like in human form.

We think about height, weight, personality, education, ambition, style, spirituality—and everything in between. Regardless of age or background, if you're single, you've likely got some version of this list. It might not be written in ink, but it's etched in the desires of your heart.

Yet for all the attention we give our lists, some critics—especially in the faith community—argue that making one reveals a lack of trust in God. They say it's superficial, restrictive, or worse, an act of self-idolatry. But let's clear the air: making a list is not about boxing God in—it's about refining your focus.

The truth is, God doesn't mind clarity. A list doesn't limit God's power—it keeps you from limiting your own standards. It sharpens your focus and keeps you from falling for "good" when God wants to give you "great."

Benefits of Your List:

1. **It keeps you aligned with your purpose.** Purpose always precedes partnership. Your calling matters more than your cravings. Marrying the wrong person can detour your destiny. Your list should reflect a standard that complements your calling, not competes with it.
2. **It keeps your emotions in check.** We've all had that moment—someone attractive walks into your life, and suddenly, logic takes a back seat. But your list? It's a reminder to stay grounded. It reminds you that attraction isn't enough. It prompts the deeper questions—"Do they support my faith? Are they emotionally healthy? Do they reflect God's heart or just good looks?"
3. **It helps you detect red flags early.** A list helps you filter with purpose. If you value honesty and emotional intelligence, but they're dishonest or emotionally manipulative, your list exposes the inconsistency. It doesn't mean you judge them—it means you guard your heart. That's not arrogance. That's wisdom.
4. **It protects your time and your peace.** There's nothing worse than investing six months in someone only to realize they never aligned with your vision. A list acts like a compass—it helps you evaluate sooner rather than later.
5. **It preserves your heart.** Relationships can either build you up or break you down. A list isn't just about filtering people out—it's about protecting your heart from unnecessary wear and tear.

Quick Sidebar: How Do I Discover My Purpose?

Your purpose is often wrapped up in what you do naturally and passionately. What energizes you? What are you good at that others find difficult? What do people thank you for? Your purpose and your partner should complement one another. Purpose without alignment will always lead to frustration.

After writing your list, break it into two sections:

- **Non-negotiables**: These are your must-haves (e.g., a deep love for God, integrity, emotional maturity, the ability to communicate well).
- **Preferences**: These are things that would be nice, but aren't deal-breakers (e.g., hair color, specific job titles, or favorite hobbies).

Your list isn't a demand letter—it's a faith-filled vision statement. It's your letter to God saying, "Lord, I trust You, but I also want to be honest about the desires You placed in my heart."

Philippians 4:6 says, *"Let your requests be made known unto God."* That includes relationship requests. God honors faith that's paired with specificity.

Become the List

You must become what you want to attract.

MARSHALL SYLVER,
Motivational Speaker

Here's where the rubber meets the road: After you've created your list, you have to ask yourself a crucial question—*Are you the kind of person your dream spouse is praying for?*

Jeremy Sanford

It's easy to demand excellence, integrity, and purpose in someone else—but are you cultivating those things in yourself?

Ladies, if your list includes a man who is spiritual, generous, and emotionally available, ask yourself: *Am I becoming the kind of woman that such a man would be drawn to—not just physically, but emotionally and spiritually?* Are you walking in the fullness of your purpose, or simply waiting to be chosen?

Gentlemen, if you desire a woman who is virtuous, driven, and spiritually mature, you must be the kind of man who brings vision, stability, and love to the table. If she's working on a doctorate and walking in purpose, she's not going to be attracted to someone who lacks discipline or drive.

Become what you pray for.

A quick PSA to the ladies: Men categorize women into two buckets—girlfriend material and wife material. One is fun; the other is foundational. One is temporary; the other is transformational. If you want to be a wife, you must carry yourself like one—before he ever puts a ring on it.

Men, the same goes for you. The kind of woman who is worth building a life with isn't impressed with talk. She wants a man with vision, discipline, and emotional presence. Be the man who doesn't just say where he's going—but has the receipts to prove it.

In Your Waiting, Give Thanks

Anyone too busy to say thank you will get fewer and fewer chances to say it.

HARVEY MACKAY
Businessman and Author

Gratitude is the door that swings wide open to blessing. Think about it: Have you ever given someone a thoughtful gift and they didn't even say thank you? Felt pretty lousy, didn't it?

Now think of how God feels when we ask for a spouse, but don't take time to thank Him for the things He's already given us. If we don't learn to praise Him in the hallway, we'll never appreciate the doors He opens.

Gratitude reframes your waiting season. It shifts your focus from what's missing to what's already meaningful. When you give thanks, you remind your soul that God's track record is flawless, and if He hasn't done it yet, it's because He's still perfecting it.

Philippians 4:6 reminds us: *"Be careful for nothing; but in everything by prayer and supplication with thanksgiving let your requests be made known unto God."* Before you ask God for a husband or wife, stop and say thank you for health, peace, provision, and protection. Gratitude doesn't delay blessings—it accelerates them.

Before you close this chapter, let me encourage you with this: Your list is not just a wishlist. It's a spiritual declaration. It's a reminder of what you're believing for. And if you're bold enough to write it down, be bold enough to become it.

And always—at the very bottom of your list—write this final line:

"If it be the Lord's will."

Because while your list is valuable, God's will is perfect. Trust Him to add, adjust, or exceed your expectations.

Scriptural Reflection

"Let your requests be made known unto God."
—Philippians 4:6

This scripture isn't a suggestion—it's an invitation. God welcomes your clarity. He desires your honesty. He delights in specificity. When you hand Him your list, with thanksgiving in your heart, He takes it—and gives you more than you ever imagined. Trust Him. He knows what you wrote, and He knows what you really need.

CHAPTER

11

Are they out of my League?

You are a living magnet. What you attract into your life is in harmony with your dominant thoughts.

BRIAN TRACY
International motivational speaker & best-selling author

It's a Saturday afternoon. You spot someone stunning across the street or seated just a few tables away at a restaurant. Almost instinctively, your mind begins to race—"Are they out of my league?" Without knowing a single detail about their heart, dreams, or values, we often sabotage ourselves in under thirty seconds.

Why? Because many of us have subconsciously categorized ourselves into levels. We've calculated—wrongly—that others are superior, more accomplished, more desirable. But here's the truth: **no one is out of your league.**

Before you dismiss that as delusional, keep reading. I promise—by the end of this chapter, you'll see why adopting that mindset may be the one thing that saves you from missing out on something extraordinary.

YOU

- Attract what you expect,
- Reflect what you desire,
- Become what you respect,
- Mirror what you admire.

We are far too conditioned to judge by appearances. But as the saying goes, *"You can't judge a book by its cover."* A beautiful exterior is just a fraction of a person's value. God made you with intentionality, purpose, and divine value—so why would you walk like someone who isn't worthy?

Say this out loud with me: **"No one is out of my league."** Let that truth sink deep. People have preferences, yes. But preference doesn't equal superiority. You may be the juiciest, ripest apple on earth—but some folks just prefer oranges. That doesn't diminish your worth; it simply means you're not their flavor.

I remember vividly—42 days ago to be exact—I met a young lady I found incredibly attractive. Long hair, great smile, and magnetic personality. To my surprise, after striking up a conversation, I learned she had already noticed me—and found me attractive as well! Had I let insecurity stop me, I would've missed that connection entirely.

On the flip side, I've also had women reject me (see Chapter 8). But that didn't mean they were "out of my league." It simply meant they weren't my match—and that's okay. What matters is this: **Don't disqualify yourself based on assumptions. Give yourself a shot.**

Not as Far-Fetched as You Thought

God will connect you to people you once thought were out of reach— only to discover you had more in common than you imagined.

DEVON FRANKLIN
Author & Film Producer

Still not convinced? You might say, *"So you're telling me any regular guy can date someone like Halle Berry?"* Here's the thing—it's not about celebrity status. It's about mindset and **positioning**.

You'll never reach someone you think is out of your league if you continue thinking that way. If you're pursuing someone who walks in excellence, purpose, and faith—you must step into that space as well.

Positioning isn't just about career or finances. It's about your **alignment with God**. When you are in the right posture spiritually—praying, walking in purpose, and seeking His will—you'll naturally attract others doing the same. In God's presence, you'll find the rare, the noble, and the extraordinary.

> *"Now unto him that is able to do exceedingly, abundantly above all that we ask or think..."*
> —Ephesians 3:20

Get in His presence and watch God bring people into your life that far surpass anything you could've orchestrated alone.

"Go where few go, and you'll find what few ever find."

Walk with Confidence

The most beautiful thing you can wear is confidence.

BLAKE LIVELY
Actress

We've all seen it—someone who looks average with a spouse who turns heads. And we wonder, *"How did they pull that off?"* The answer: **confidence**.

Confidence is not arrogance; it's a deep inner belief that you bring something valuable to the table. Confidence says, *"I know who I am, I know whose I am, and I know what I deserve."*

What are your strengths? Do you make people laugh? Cook well? Have a strong work ethic or a passionate dream that will change your community? These are all attractive traits—and they matter far more than just looks.

"As a man thinketh in his heart, so is he."
—Proverbs 23:7

Your self-perception shapes your reality. If you believe you're a six, that energy will radiate. But someone else may see you as a ten—if only you believed it yourself.

Beauty is in the eye of the beholder. Your past may have made you doubt your worth—but the right person won't see your scars, only your strength. So, walk boldly. And don't let past rejections write the narrative for your future.

Go for the Best

Shoot for the moon. Even if you miss, you'll land among the stars.

LES BROWN
Motivational Speaker

What's the point of settling for someone who doesn't excite you? If you're going to pursue a lifelong relationship, **go for someone who makes your heart race and your spirit soar.**

Don't just marry someone because your parents or friends think they're nice. Marry someone who feels like a gift from God. Someone you're proud to be seen with, talk about, and dream with.

True story: When I was 18, I dated a 24-year-old woman. She was kind and liked me a lot. But I wasn't genuinely excited about her. Over time, my lack of emotional investment became obvious—and ultimately my lack of interest hurt her. That experience taught me a lesson I now live by: **If your heart isn't fully in it, don't get in it at all.**

Don't commit out of boredom, pressure, or fear of being alone. Only commit when your spirit leaps at the thought of building something amazing with that person.

And one final note to the ladies: stop pursuing men. You weren't designed to hunt—you were designed to be **chosen**. Men were made to pursue. When a man doesn't chase you, something is off. Let him initiate. If he's not hunting, he either isn't ready or isn't the one.

FINAL WORD: Kingdom Confidence

In the kingdom of God, *"out of your league"* doesn't exist. When you walk with God, *you* become the league.

So next time you see someone who takes your breath away, don't shrink. Don't replay your past. Just smile, remember who you are in Christ, and trust that if it's God's will—it's already yours.

> *"With God, all things are possible."*
> —Matthew 19:26

CHAPTER

12

Ask sooner

You are a living magnet. What you attract into your life is in harmony with your dominant thoughts.

BRIAN TRACY
International motivational speaker & best-selling author

Time Is Priceless. Don't Waste It.

If money is a currency, then time is a treasure—and once it's spent, it can never be recovered. Whether you're currently dating or looking forward to meeting someone soon, one of the wisest things you can do is **ask better questions sooner**. Why? Because time is too sacred to waste on people going nowhere slowly.

Ephesians 5:15–16 says,

> *"Be very careful, then, how you live—not as unwise but as wise, making the most of every opportunity, because the days are evil."*

In other words: Don't date blindly. Ask boldly.

Admire Less, Investigate More

It's easy to admire someone when you're attracted to them. But dating is not just about admiration—it's about **evaluation**. Don't spend all your time admiring their dimples, their job title, or the fact that they love the same TV shows as you. That's cute—but it won't hold a marriage together.

Ask the questions that count:

- What motivates you every morning?
- Do you pray daily?
- What does "a successful marriage" look like to you?
- How do you respond to conflict?

The more clarity you get early on, the less heartbreak you experience later.

90 Days of Clarity

Relationship coach Tony Gaskins says you should be able to **fully evaluate** someone within 90 days. That doesn't mean rush into a relationship, but it does mean you can make an informed decision about whether to continue.

Too many singles waste **years** because they didn't want to ask the hard questions. Remember: A breakup after 3 months stings. A breakup after 3 years scars.

> *"Guard your heart above all else, for it determines the course of your life."*
> —Proverbs 4:23 (NLT)

Don't just guard your heart with time—guard it with truth.

Ask the Right Questions

Some questions are charming... but empty.
"Favorite color?"
"Cats or dogs?"
"Mountains or beach?"

Cute? Yes.
Crucial? Not even close.

Instead, ask questions that reveal character, convictions, and calling. The right questions uncover what years of casual conversation will never tell you.

And if their answers are **vague**, don't settle.

Don't Accept Vague Answers

A vague answer is not a red flag—it's a stop sign.
When someone tells you, "I'm almost finished with school," but can't tell you what school, what degree, or what semester they're in... pause. Clarify.

It's not about being pushy. It's about being **purposeful**.

Luke 6:45 says,

> *"Out of the abundance of the heart, the mouth speaks."*

If you ask clearly and they still speak vaguely, chances are they aren't ready for the level of relationship you're pursuing.

Skeletons vs. Truth

Many people avoid asking real questions because they're afraid of uncovering something that may force them to walk away. But ignoring red flags doesn't make them disappear—it just delays the damage.

Here's the truth: **Asking doesn't ruin relationships. Avoiding does.**
You're not being judgmental—you're being intentional.

Protect Your Present, Honor Your Future

When you ask the right questions early, you **protect your heart** and **honor your future spouse**. God is not just preparing someone for you—He's preparing **you** for someone. The only way to step into that promise is by **refusing to waste time on counterfeits.**

If God has someone incredible waiting to meet you, why waste months (or years) with someone who never should've had that access in the first place?

Scriptural Reflection

> *"For everything there is a season, a time for every activity under heaven… a time to search and a time to quit searching."*
> —Ecclesiastes 3:1, 6 (NLT)

Don't let fear or fantasy delay your destiny.
Ask sooner.
Ask deeper.
Ask wisely.

Because every question you ask is a step toward the clarity God desires you to walk in.

CHAPTER

13

Cleanse Yourself

*Do not sabotage your new relationship with
your last relationship's poison.*

STEVE MARABOLI
Keynote Speaker, Bestselling Author, and philanthropist

SECTION ONE: Broken Hearts, Hidden Fears

There's a condition many carry—often silently—called **pistanthrophobia**: the fear of trusting others because of past relational wounds. You may not be able to pronounce it, but chances are, you've felt it. It's that knot in your stomach that whispers: *Don't trust again—it'll only hurt worse next time.*

You gave your heart. You loved hard. But they didn't love you back the same way—or worse, they betrayed you. Now you're left picking up the pieces of what should've been a beautiful story. If you're honest, you've spent nights crying, wondering how someone who knew your heart could be so careless with it.

You're not alone—and you're not weak. You're just human.
But here's the truth: **God does not waste pain.** He transforms it. If you let Him, He'll use it to heal you, teach you, and prepare you.

Pain Can't Stay Forever

You may want to avoid love altogether. You've told yourself it's safer to stay single than risk another emotional collapse. But pain is a *visitor*, not a *resident*. It cannot and will not stay forever.

> *"Weeping may endure for a night, but joy comes in the morning."*
> —Psalm 30:5

God promises not only to heal the wound but to restore the joy. He'll redeem the tears you cried in secret and replace them with laughter and peace. How do I know? Because He's done it for me.

Joseph's Blueprint for Healing

Consider Joseph. Betrayed by his own brothers. Thrown into a pit. Sold into slavery. Left alone. Forgotten. Yet, through it all, **God was with him**.

He could have turned bitter. He could've vowed never to trust again. Instead, he leaned into purpose and allowed time, obedience, and God's favor to do the healing.

Years later, he didn't just forgive his brothers—he *blessed* them. That's the kind of healing only God can produce. And He wants to do the same in your life.

If Joseph can heal from betrayal by blood, you can heal from betrayal by romance. But it starts with letting go—and letting God.

No Carry-Ons Allowed

Healing is a decision before it becomes a feeling.
You can't board your next relationship flight with unresolved baggage. This is a **no carry-on zone**. If you want to soar, you must travel light.

Don't punish your next person for the pain your last person caused. They didn't hurt you. They didn't lie to you. They haven't broken your trust—yet. Let them show you who they are without the shadow of someone they've never met.

A clean slate is a gift.
Offer it—and expect it in return.

Beyond Stereotypes

It's easy to start believing lies when you've been hurt.
"All men cheat."
"All women are crazy."
"All relationships end in pain."

These aren't facts. They're fear-based generalizations. Don't let stereotypes become your belief system. Not all men are dogs. Not all women are dramatic. And not all love stories are doomed to fail.

There are good people in this world—faithful, loving, healed people—who are praying for someone just like you. But they can only find the real you, not the guarded version of you. So drop the labels, release the lies, and open your heart again.

Ready to Sacrifice?

Before you step into a new relationship, ask yourself: *Am I ready to serve someone other than myself?*

Relationships are partnerships. Teams. Two people who learn to prioritize each other's needs even when it's inconvenient.

Love isn't built on butterflies—it's built on **sacrifice**:

- Staying off the phone so they can study.
- Forgiving misunderstandings and miscommunications.
- Listening when it's easier to interrupt.

Sacrifice is not always about grand gestures—it's often shown in small moments of understanding.

Listen First, Love Second

Most arguments don't start with betrayal. They start with **perspective gaps** and a lack of listening.

Real listening isn't waiting for your turn to speak.
It's hearing their heart—even when you disagree.
It's picking up the hints, the silence, the stories between the lines.

Men: if she says she's running low on perfume three times in a week, that's not random—it's a request.

Ladies: if he says he doesn't like aprons, please don't get him one for Christmas and then wonder why he's distant.

Want fewer arguments?
Listen more. Defend less. Understand deeper.

Trust Must Be the Foundation

No matter how great the connection, if trust is shaky, the entire relationship will eventually collapse.

Trust doesn't mean ignoring red flags. It means evaluating character and, when you find consistency, choosing to believe the best—until proven otherwise.

Let God do the heart-mending first. Otherwise, you'll enter with fear instead of faith. And fear has no place in a love story God is writing.

Scriptural Reflection

> *"And the God of all grace, who called you to His eternal glory in Christ, after you have suffered a little while, will Himself restore you and make you strong, firm and steadfast."*
>
> —1 Peter 5:10

Your past doesn't disqualify you—it **prepares** you.
Your brokenness isn't the end of your story—it's the start of your healing. Let God restore, renew, and realign your heart so it's ready to receive what He's already prepared for you.

Your person exists. They're living, breathing, walking this Earth right now. But they're not your assignment until your heart is healed.

So, before you pursue your next, ask God to cleanse your now.

CHAPTER

14

Love before First Sight

I believe that two people are connected at the heart, and it doesn't matter what you do, or who you are or where you live; there are no boundaries or barriers if two people are destined to be together.

JULIA ROBERTS
American Actress and Producer

Have you ever felt the echo of something you couldn't see yet—something so real, so specific, it almost felt like déjà vu? A presence in your spirit. A soft whisper that says, "Get ready. Everything is about to change."

This chapter isn't about love at first sight.

It's about something far more mysterious, more intentional.

It's about love *before* first sight.

The Weight of Waiting

For eight straight years, I attended the PCAF National Convention. Eight years. Every summer, I showed up full of faith and fire. I came to grow, to serve, to worship—and, if I'm honest, to look.

Not just for any woman. I wasn't chasing affection. I was searching for alignment.

Each year brought new faces—women who were kind, intelligent, even breathtaking. But as great as they were, there was always something missing. A hesitation in my spirit. A check in my soul. I didn't want chemistry without calling. I didn't want compatibility without covenant.

It's a strange tension—to be fulfilled in your purpose, but still feel the silent ache of relational anticipation. I knew I was called. I knew I was whole. And still, I knew there was a missing piece only heaven could deliver.

And then came 2016.

I wasn't expecting anything that year. I had almost written it off. The convention was in Detroit, Michigan, and I arrived with my usual rhythm—connect with friends, attend the sessions, support the movement, and return home. No expectations.

But when you least expect it, God has a way of unfolding destiny in plain sight.

An Unexpected Introduction

After lunch with a few close friends near the riverfront, I found myself wandering through the convention center, casually stepping into a business session—not for the content, but to pass the time.

That's when I heard someone call out, "What's up, Pastor J?"

I turned—and that's when I saw her.

Zaria.

Her hair flowed like time slowed for her alone. There was a quiet strength in her posture, a poise that stood out without asking for attention. And then there was her smile—warm, effortless, sincere. The kind that doesn't just light up a room; it softens it.

She was from New Jersey.

I introduced myself with my usual confidence, but inside, something in me whispered, "This is not a moment to let pass."

So I circled back.

"Wait, tell me your name again?" I asked.

"Zaria," she said with a soft laugh.

There it was. That name would linger in my mind for the rest of the day… and the rest of my life.

We had an effortless conversation—no nerves, no pretenses. Just flow. And when I asked for her number, she smiled, took my phone, and entered it in.

I walked away not with butterflies, but with peace. Not with euphoria, but with assurance.

I didn't know how it would all play out—but I knew something had just shifted.

Before Sight, There Was Prayer

It wasn't until later that I learned Zaria had noticed me before.

One year earlier.

At the **exact same convention**, held in Jacksonville, Florida. She spotted me in a crowd and leaned over to her cousin. "He's cute," she whispered. Her mom, sitting nearby, noticed her reaction and discreetly took a few photos of me on her phone.

They never spoke to me. I never saw them. But a seed had been planted.

And exactly **one year to the day**, that seed bloomed.

Now, tell me that's coincidence.

Better yet—tell me that's not God.

Divine Timing Is Better Than Perfect Timing

Love at first sight? I absolutely believe in it! You've got to keep the faith. Who doesn't like the idea that you could see someone tomorrow and she could be the love of your life? It's very romantic.

LEONARDO DICAPRIO

I believe in divine interruptions—those moments when God steps into your regularly scheduled life and rewrites the script. That meeting with Zaria wasn't on my calendar. It wasn't planned or pursued. But it was **aligned**.

Love doesn't always rush in with fireworks. Sometimes, it walks in like a whisper—just loud enough for your spirit to hear.

Intentionality Over Infatuation

Over the next 90 days, I didn't rush. I watched. I listened. I prayed.

We talked regularly—sometimes light, sometimes deep. I asked questions about her values, her vision, her past, her faith. And what I learned was undeniable.

She had depth. Emotional intelligence. A calming presence. Zaria wasn't loud or overbearing, but she didn't shrink either. She was secure. And wise.

Every time I tried to mentally box her into the "just a friend" category, something inside pushed back. She was **more**.

The Visit That Changed Everything

That Thanksgiving, I flew to see her. Her family welcomed me with kindness—but not softness. They were protective. I didn't mind it. In fact, I respected it.

We spent the weekend talking by the water, exploring the city, laughing over meals, and doing something that stretched me beyond my comfort zone—zip-lining.

There's something about seeing someone outside their routine. How they handle fear. How they process stress. How they react when plans shift.

Zaria was composed. Joyful. Present.

When it was time for me to head back home, I hugged her goodbye and drove off.

Later that night, I sat in my room, scrolling through photos from the weekend.

And I cried.

Not tears of confusion or regret. These were tears of clarity.

I knew.

A Letter from Before the Beginning

Weeks later, Zaria showed me something sacred.

It was a letter she had written to God almost a year before we met. In it, she poured her heart out, detailing the kind of love she hoped for, the kind of man she believed God would send.

She didn't just write about romance—she wrote about **responsibility**.

"I promise to cover him in prayer.
I promise to support his calling.
I promise to love him unconditionally.
I promise to honor what you've placed in him."

Reading her words wrecked me. Because while I was praying for a wife, she was praying for a husband—and our prayers were aimed in the same direction.

We didn't find each other by accident.

We were being led to each other on purpose.

Love That Waits Is Love That's Worth It

We live in a world where everything is rushed. Fast food. Fast Wi-Fi. Fast love.

But anything built to last is built with patience. God isn't in a hurry—He's into alignment. While you're waiting, He's working. While you're trusting, He's orchestrating.

Zaria wasn't just an answer to a prayer. She was the **fulfillment** of a process. The culmination of patience. The reward of faith.

Every missed connection before her made sense now.

When God Confirms, Peace Follows

I never had to force it with Zaria.

I didn't have to chase her, convince her, or mold her. I just had to show up as my full, healed self—and so did she.

When God is in something, peace shows up like a silent witness.

It doesn't mean there's no uncertainty—but even the uncertainty doesn't rattle you. You move with peace in your steps and clarity in your heart.

Scriptural Reflection

"Delight yourself also in the Lord, and He shall give you the desires of your heart."
—Psalm 37:4 (NKJV)

This verse doesn't promise that God will hand us every wish like a genie. It's deeper than that.

When you delight yourself in Him—when your joy is rooted in who He is, not just what He can give—He begins to shape your desires. Align them. Refine them. And in His time, He brings you into alignment with the very things He planted in your heart to begin with.

Zaria wasn't just the desire of my heart—she was the **fruit** of my delight in God.

So if you're still waiting—keep delighting.

If you're still healing—keep hoping.

If you're still believing—keep building your life.

Because love doesn't always come wrapped in the timing you want.

But it **always** comes wrapped in the timing you need.

CHAPTER

15

Let The Guns Blaze

Two things remain irretrievable: time and first impressions.
CYNTHIA OZICK

Meeting your partner's parents is one of the most critical moments in any serious relationship. It is a milestone that marks the crossing from casual affection into something sacred and serious. When your significant other invites you into their family circle, it signals trust, respect, and the hope that you will eventually be woven into the fabric of their shared history.

This is a threshold moment—one that demands your best self, your most genuine heart, and an awareness that the stakes are higher than just a first impression. The parents you meet are more than just family—they are gatekeepers of the legacy you are hoping to join. They carry the weight of their child's past and future on their shoulders, and meeting you is their opportunity to see if you are worthy of standing alongside their beloved.

The Weight of Legacy

Parents don't just open their doors for any person who crosses their child's path. They open their homes for those who hold promise, who embody integrity, and who can offer a vision for the future—a future they want their child to share. The sacrifices they've made—the long nights, the worries, the tears, the celebrations—are all wrapped up in their protective instincts.

When you step into their world, you enter a sacred space filled with hopes, dreams, and unspoken prayers for the one they love most. You're not just meeting a couple of people—you're meeting the very roots of your partner's existence. And how you carry yourself here can either strengthen or fracture the fragile trust that is being built.

This moment is an invitation to **let the guns blaze**—not in confrontation, but in authenticity, courage, and boldness. This is your chance to show that you are someone who doesn't shy away from responsibility, who can be trusted, and who values the relationship enough to stand tall in the face of scrutiny.

What Parents Really Want to See

There's a common misconception that parents are only looking for perfection or for you to meet some impossible checklist. The truth is far more human and simpler: parents want to see **value**. They want to witness your character in action, your intentions clearly stated, and your willingness to love their child with respect and honor.

They want assurance that you will be a partner in life's joys and challenges—that you'll uplift rather than tear down. They want to see your potential, your purpose, and your resolve. They want to know that their child will be safe and cherished, not only today but decades from now.

And so, when you enter that room, carry yourself with a quiet confidence. Speak truthfully about your goals and dreams. Show respect through your words and actions. Listen deeply to their stories and wisdom. When the guns blaze, let it be with the fire of integrity and love.

The Nerves Are Real—But So Is the Opportunity

Nerves before meeting the parents are natural. The stakes feel high because, in many ways, they are. But don't let fear lead you into inauthenticity or hesitation. This moment is also a tremendous opportunity—a door to deeper connection and trust.

I remember the night I met Zaria's parents like it was yesterday. It was a warm Thanksgiving evening filled with laughter and chatter. Walking into their home, I was immediately aware of all eyes on me—some curious, some cautious. Their smiles were welcoming but measured, as if silently asking, "Who is this man, and what does he want from our daughter?"

The initial conversation was a dance—questions exchanged carefully; stories shared with measured candor. When Zaria's father looked me squarely in the eyes and asked, "What are your intentions with my daughter?" my heart thundered. But I answered simply and honestly, "I want to get to know her better and build a meaningful friendship."

That moment was the beginning—not the end. Meeting the parents isn't about winning an instant approval but about opening a door to ongoing respect, understanding, and patience.

Dress Nicely

The way you dress is the billboard that tells perceptive people how you feel about yourself.

BARBARA WALTERS

Appearance is the silent language that speaks before words can. When you meet your partner's parents, your attire conveys a message about who you are, what you value, and how seriously you take this relationship.

This doesn't mean dressing like you're walking the red carpet or stepping onto a fashion runway. But it does mean **intentionality**—showing up clean, neat, and respectful of the occasion.

What to Wear: The Unspoken Rules

For gentlemen, a crisp, collared shirt with dark, well-fitted jeans or slacks often strikes the perfect balance between casual and respectful. Avoid anything too flashy or too worn. Clean shoes and groomed hair are a must; they show you care about the impression you make.

Ladies should consider attire that is tasteful and modest without sacrificing style. A well-chosen dress or blouse and skirt combo that fits well and respects the family setting sends the message that you take the meeting seriously. Avoid anything too revealing or overly casual like ripped jeans or loud prints.

Remember, parents are protective. They want to feel their child is respected by the company they keep. Your clothes can either open doors to trust or close them before you even speak.

More Than Clothes

Appearance is only part of the picture. Equally important is how you carry yourself—the posture, the smile, the eye contact, and the tone of your voice. Walk in with confidence tempered by humility. Greet each person with warmth and sincerity. Show that you're interested, not only in impressing but in truly connecting.

Parents want to hear about your dreams and goals. Don't be afraid to share your vision, whether you're working full-time, in school, or building a business. They want to see purpose and ambition—not perfection, but direction.

Speak clearly and authentically about your future plans. Let them see that you are committed to growth, stability, and partnership.

The Power of Respect and Intentionality

When you show up dressed nicely and prepared to engage respectfully, you demonstrate more than good manners—you show that you understand the importance of this union. This is a small but powerful way to honor your partner and their family.

Respect is not a one-time event but a lifestyle. Dressing well for this meeting is your first opportunity to lay a foundation of respect that will carry through every interaction to come.

Entering Into the Unknown

The night I met Zaria's parents was one of nervous anticipation mixed with hopeful excitement. Their home was filled with family members celebrating her birthday and the Thanksgiving holiday. I felt the weight of every glance, every smile, every question.

The conversation flowed between casual banter and serious inquiries. Zaria's father's question about my intentions was a defining moment. I could see that what mattered most wasn't my words alone but the sincerity behind them.

I also remember the moment he asked if I was willing to wait two years while Zaria finished school. I answered without hesitation—because honesty was my only option. The answer was not just to appease him but a reflection of the commitment I was willing to make.

Meeting the parents is entering into the unknown with courage, vulnerability, and respect. It's stepping into a new chapter, not knowing exactly how it will unfold but trusting that your genuine heart will guide the way.

Scriptural Reflection

"Honor your father and your mother, so that your days may be long in the land that the Lord your God is giving you."

—Exodus 20:12 (NIV)

This commandment is one of the pillars of godly living. It is more than an instruction—it is a promise of blessing and longevity. When you meet your partner's parents, you have an opportunity to live out this command in a tangible way.

Honoring parents means more than just polite words. It means showing respect for the foundation they have laid and seeking their blessing with humility. It means acknowledging the sacredness of family and recognizing that relationships don't exist in isolation but within a web of connection ordained by God.

When you approach this meeting with a heart of honor, you step into a divine rhythm that invites blessing, peace, and favor. The journey of love is intertwined with the legacy of family—and when we honor that, we position ourselves to build a future rooted in faith, respect, and grace.

CHAPTER

16

The War Within

The most difficult war is the fight within yourself

ANIL B VEDMEHTA

CEO of global manufacturing and consulting company

Warning: This chapter is not for the faint of heart.
If you're looking for fluff, feel-good vibes, or a surface-level conversation—this isn't it. But if you've ever been in a relationship where your body wanted one thing, your mind said it wasn't a big deal, and your spirit whispered, *"Not yet"*—then this chapter is for you.

Let's talk about the war that too many people pretend doesn't exist: the war within.

In a love relationship, especially one with deep emotional and physical chemistry, one of the hardest things to control is your sexual passion. Let's not sugarcoat it: **humans want sex.** It's how we're wired. God, in His infinite wisdom, designed us that way.

He made man to be drawn to woman. Woman to be drawn to man. He crafted our bodies to respond—chemically, emotionally, biologically—to each other. He created us with every tool necessary to experience intimacy, connection, and gratification.

But here's where it gets challenging: while we have the capacity to express love physically, God's word places *timing* and *contextual boundaries* on how and when that love should be expressed.

Sex was created for the covenant of marriage. Period.

And yet, God also created you to feel these desires—sometimes strongly, intensely, and frequently—*before* marriage. Why? Because He wants your relationship with Him and your partner to be one of trust, obedience, and spiritual growth, not just emotional and physical release.

It's the ultimate paradox.
It's the war within.

When a Hug Isn't Enough

There are seasons when a hug just won't do. When you're falling in love with someone who loves you back, your mind begins to search for ways to show it. When the chemistry is undeniable, even innocent physical touch begins to feel like fire.

And let's be honest:
You don't stop wanting sex just because you love Jesus.

Even if you fast three times a week. Even if you lead worship or preach sermons. Even if you post scriptures on social media and your Bible app streak is 120 days long—**you are still human.**

Your spirit may be saved, but your body didn't get the memo.

And when your flesh starts craving what your faith says you can't have yet, you realize just how real the fight is.

The temptation isn't just physical—it's psychological and emotional. You start rationalizing. You start compromising.

"God knows my heart..."

"We're going to get married anyway..."

"I love them. Isn't that what matters?"

And yet, in the depths of your soul, the Spirit says: *Wait.*

Not because God is cruel.

Not because He wants to rob you of joy.

But because He wants your joy to be *complete*.

I Want It So Bad

Your worst battle is between what you know and what you feel.

UNKNOWN

Lust is a wild animal. And if you don't tame it, it will tame you.

The longer you're around someone you're attracted to, the more your physical desires come alive. You want to kiss them. You want to touch them. You want to be in their arms and express your love with everything inside you.

Listen, I've been there.

Not just once. Not just in theory. I'm 28 years old. I've never been married. And no, I'm not a virgin. But I've been **celibate for 9 years.**

Nine.

That's almost a decade of choosing God's standard over my desires. A decade of saying "no" to late-night text invites, temptation in college dorm rooms, flirtations at work, and everything in between.

It hasn't been easy. But it has been worth it.

I made a vow at 19 when God changed my life. After receiving the Holy Spirit and committing my life to Christ, I walked away from things that were dragging me down—**including fornication.** And that decision has changed everything.

Since then, God has blessed me more than I could imagine.
I drive my dream car.
I live in a beautiful home.
I hold three degrees and work in a high-paying role.
But none of that is the *why*.

I didn't do it for the blessings.
I did it because I fell in love with Jesus.

Don't Serve God for What He Can Give You

If your commitment to God is rooted in what He can do for you, that commitment won't last. Because eventually the blessings will delay or disappear, and you'll be left with a faith that can't stand without rewards.

But when your love for God is rooted in gratitude—
In the fact that He saved you, redeemed you, forgave you, and called you—then you serve Him even when it's hard. Even when it hurts. Even when it's lonely.

Has it been a perfect journey? Absolutely not.
Have there been moments where temptation was so thick I could barely breathe? Yes.

I've had women approach me with offers that many guys would've taken without blinking. "So, you don't have sex?" they'd ask. Some were genuinely curious. Others were mocking. "Are you gay?" "You serious?" "Why would you wait?"

My response has always been simple:
"I'm doing this because I made a commitment to God. I'm waiting for marriage. That's the standard I believe in."

The awkward silence that followed? I've gotten used to it.
The ridicule? I've grown past it.
The temptation? I still feel it—but I don't let it rule me.

Because I've learned that **your body may want it, but your soul wants something deeper.**

Two Keys to Sexual Self-Control

Let's get practical. Because spiritual clichés won't help when your hormones are doing backflips and your favorite worship playlist isn't calming you down.

Here are the two keys that have helped me stay sexually pure for nearly a decade:

1. Harness Your Desires

Sexual desire isn't a sin. Acting on it outside of God's timing is. Passion is a powerful force—but like fire, if you don't place it in the right container, it will burn everything in sight.

You can't kill your sexual appetite, but you *can* train it.
The more you feed it, the more it grows.
The more you starve it in unhealthy contexts, the more it becomes manageable.

Your body isn't in charge—**your spirit is.**

2. Stay Out of Traps

This one is simple: if you don't want to fall, stop walking near the edge.

Don't Netflix and chill in dim lighting.
Don't spend the night at each other's place "just to talk."
Don't assume you're stronger than you are.

You don't resist temptation by *flexing* your willpower. You resist it by fleeing. If Joseph had stayed in Potiphar's house, he would've slept with Potiphar's wife. Period. But he RAN.

You don't play with fire and pray not to get burned.

Fast Forward: The Power of Fasting

There's a weapon in your spiritual arsenal that most people overlook: **fasting.**

Fasting isn't just about food. It's about focus.
When you fast, you remind your body that it doesn't run the show. You quiet your flesh so that your spirit can speak louder.

When I fast, I go from midnight to 4 p.m. without food or water. During that time, I cut out entertainment and social media. I open my Bible, spend time in prayer, and ask God to strengthen me.

And every time I do, I come out more focused. More centered. More obedient.

Fasting is spiritual resistance training.
It builds spiritual strength.

Trust God's Timing

Here's the truth most people don't want to admit: if you step outside of God's timing for sex, it won't just damage your relationship—it will delay your blessings.

God doesn't give us rules to control us. He gives us boundaries to *protect us*.
To preserve our joy.
To position us for lasting love.

And when you wait, when you trust Him, when you hold the line even when everything in you wants to cross it—**God honors that.**

Not just with stuff, but with peace.
With clarity.
With a future worth waiting for.

Final Thoughts

This war within—it's not for the weak.
But you're not weak.

God created you to overcome temptation, not by pretending it doesn't exist, but by confronting it with *spirit-filled strategy.*

If you're in a season of dating or waiting, I want to encourage you: you're not alone. You're not broken for having desires. You're not crazy for choosing God's way.

In fact, you're **brave.**

Hold the line.
Harness your desires.

Stay out of the trap.
Fast when it gets intense.
Pray like your future depends on it—because it does.

Scriptural Reflection

> *"So I say, walk by the Spirit, and you will not gratify the desires of the flesh. For the flesh desires what is contrary to the Spirit, and the Spirit what is contrary to the flesh."*
> —Galatians 5:16–17 (NIV)

This verse doesn't promise that the battle will be easy. It promises that victory is possible when you *walk by the Spirit.*

You were never meant to win this war alone.
Let the Spirit of God guide you.
Let Him fight for you.
Let Him fill the empty spaces that lust tries to occupy.

And remember:
Obedience may cost you something in the moment,
but it brings *everything* in the end.

CHAPTER

17

Love worth Fighting for

Whenever you're in conflict with someone, there is one factor that can make the difference between damaging your relationship or deepening it. That factor is attitude.

WILLIAM JAMES
American philosopher and psychologist

If I wrote an entire book on love and never mentioned that it takes effort, I would be doing you a disservice.

Because love—real, covenant-level love—is not passive. It doesn't coast on good days or crumble under pressure. It fights. It endures. It leans in when it would be easier to walk away. That kind of love? It's not only worth having—it's worth fighting for.

It's easy to romanticize love. Hollywood tells us that if it's hard, it must not be right. But here's the truth: even the strongest, most God-ordained relationships go through storms. Two people can be deeply in love and still have conflict. Why? Because men and women are designed differently—on purpose. We are wired for connection, but we are also wired for contrast. That contrast can be beautiful when embraced and brutal when ignored.

Conflict, then, is not a sign that something is wrong. It's a sign that something is real.

The Misunderstood Power of Conflict

Let's be clear—conflict, in and of itself, is not the enemy. Unresolved conflict is. Swept-under-the-rug conflict is. Passive-aggressive silence and emotional stonewalling are. Conflict that is never addressed becomes corrosive.

I want to help you see conflict for what it truly is: an opportunity. A doorway to deeper understanding, greater intimacy, and lasting growth—if you approach it the right way.

How you *handle* conflict determines the health of your relationship more than whether you *have* conflict at all.

Some couples pretend everything is fine when it's not. They hope the issue will disappear like a puff of smoke. But this isn't magic. Conflict doesn't vanish; it festers. It becomes the elephant in the room—growing bigger and louder until it crashes through your peace like a wrecking ball.

Unaddressed conflict is like weeds in your front yard. You can mow over them and pretend they're gone, but unless you dig out the root, they'll return—stronger, uglier, and more stubborn.

You don't have to fear conflict. You just have to learn to fight right.

Conflict Starts Small

Let me paint a picture. Joanna asks Peter to take out the trash. He forgets. She reminds him again—"Babe, I told you yesterday to take out the trash. You never listen!" That one word—*never*—is a spark. Peter, already exhausted from a long day, hears it as an insult. It feels like an accusation, not a reminder.

So what happens? He responds defensively: "I don't always forget. And if you saw it was full, why didn't you take it out?"

Now they're both on edge, and the conversation quickly escalates. What started as a small, solvable issue becomes a breeding ground for resentment.

Let me offer some practical wisdom here: when arguing, avoid using absolutes like *never* or *always*. These words invite past offenses into the present moment and make your partner feel like their efforts are being erased.

A disagreement over trash turns into a trial about character, responsibility, and whether they're appreciated in the relationship. Not because of the trash—but because of the tone.

Respond with Grace, Not Guard

The next time you're tempted to snap back, pause. Ask yourself, "Is this a moment to defend or to understand?"

If you know the person you're with loves you—and they know you love them—then lead with that foundation. Assume the best. Respond with grace, not a guarded heart.

Here's a healthier way that same conflict could go:

Joanna: "Babe, I asked about the trash yesterday and it's still full. I know you're probably tired, but can you please handle it before bed?"

Peter: "You're right—I totally forgot. That's on me. I'll take care of it now. Thanks for the reminder."

No explosion. No bruised egos. Just honesty and ownership.

Communication is the Glue

If you want your relationship to survive hard seasons, you must create a culture where both people feel safe expressing themselves.

Here's the formula:

1. Communicate frequently.
2. Speak respectfully.
3. Listen deeply—especially when it's uncomfortable.

Give your partner the space to say what's on their heart without fearing judgment or defensiveness. But also, be courageous enough to say what you need to say—kindly, clearly, and without keeping score.

The goal of conflict resolution isn't winning. It's connection.

Common Sources of Conflict

You're not alone in your struggles. The most common areas couples fight about are:

- Money
- Time
- Chores
- Family
- Physical intimacy
- Work
- Parenting

None of these are inherently bad. In fact, they're simply categories where life happens. But when expectations go unspoken or boundaries are crossed, tension rises.

Life is far too short to spend it arguing. You get to decide whether your days are filled with conflict or joy. The difference lies in how quickly you choose to resolve disagreements.

A Personal Story: The Disconnect

A few months ago, I planned an entire day of fun for Zaria and me. We love sports and movement, so I set up tennis in the morning, followed by golf, then lunch.

When I picked her up that morning, I could tell something was off. Zaria is normally light, vibrant—her smile fills the room before she even walks in. But this day, her light felt dimmed.

I asked her if she was okay. She said, "Yeah, I'm fine," but her tone said otherwise.

We still had fun playing tennis, even laughed here and there. But you know how you can laugh and still feel a wall between you? That was us. I couldn't shake it.

I chalked it up to maybe being tired or maybe... *girl problems* (don't judge me). I didn't want to press, so we moved on.

At the driving range, she tried golf for the first time. I was excited—excited to teach her, to laugh, to see her competitive side. But that wall was still there. And for the first time, I felt like I couldn't reach her.

I tried to get her to open up a bit more as we walked back to the car, but even that felt different. Softer. Distant. As I got in the car, I couldn't take it anymore. I turned and said, "Honey, are you sure there's nothing wrong?"

She took a breath. "I wrote you a letter... but we'll talk about it later."

At that moment, my heart sank. The fact that she wrote a letter told me this wasn't a small thing. Something I had done had hurt her enough that she needed to process it in writing. And I didn't even know what it was.

It crushed me—but it also taught me something.

You don't always know when you've hurt the person you love. Sometimes your intent is pure, but your impact misses the mark. And sometimes, the only way to close the gap is through vulnerability, not assumption.

I had a choice in that moment. I could be defensive and say, "Why didn't you just tell me?" or I could listen and lean in.

I chose to lean in.

We talked. We healed. And we became stronger because of it.

Conflict Can Deepen Connection

Handled poorly, conflict creates distance. Handled with grace, conflict creates depth.

When you choose humility over ego, listening over arguing, and restoration over retaliation, your love matures. You become more than just a couple—you become a team.

Think of conflict as a spiritual workout. It reveals your weaknesses, yes—but it also strengthens your bond.

Let me be clear: you're not just fighting *about* something. You're fighting *for* something. You're fighting for your future. For your peace. For your purpose together.

This kind of love isn't for the faint of heart. It's for those who are willing to grow.

It's for those who understand that blessings still require maintenance. That every beautiful garden has weeds that must be pulled. That love isn't found—it's *built*.

Time is a Gift

Time is the most precious commodity you have. Don't waste it dragging out arguments that could be resolved with one honest conversation.

You can spend your days in silent treatment and tension, or you can spend them laughing, learning, and loving. The choice is yours.

I know you might feel justified in your silence. I know you might feel wounded and want them to come to you first. But what if love went first? What if *you* went first?

Even God, knowing all our faults, came to *us* first.

If He can take the first step toward reconciliation, maybe we can too.

Scriptural Reflection:

> *"If it is possible, as far as it depends on you,*
> *live at peace with everyone."*
> —Romans 12:18 (NIV)

This verse isn't just about coexisting—it's about intentional effort. *As far as it depends on you.* That means we each carry responsibility in the pursuit of peace.

When conflict comes—and it will—ask yourself: Have I done everything in my power to live in peace? Not to avoid truth, but to honor it. Not to pretend everything is fine, but to fight for what matters.

Jeremy Sanford

Fighting for love doesn't mean fighting *each other*. It means fighting *together* against the things that threaten your connection—pride, silence, assumptions, unforgiveness.

Choose peace. Choose humility. Choose to fight for the love that God gave you.

Because *love is worth fighting for.*

CHAPTER

18

A Perfect Match...Kinda

Great love isn't two people finding the perfect match in one another. Great love is two people making the choice to be a match.

LYSA TERKEURST, NYT BEST-SELLING AUTHOR

So now that you've met someone worth getting to know, or maybe even someone worth loving... where do you go from here?

I've spent the last two years writing this book—and living it. And one thing I've discovered is that finding real love takes a lot more than simply getting someone's number. You can be educated, well-dressed, and emotionally intelligent and still find yourself alone in a sea of potential partners that somehow never quite become *the one.*

I've seen this dilemma play out on both sides—brilliant, successful women wondering where all the good men are, and stable, thoughtful men struggling to find a woman who matches both their heart and their purpose.

This isn't a problem we can solve overnight, but we can make progress by acknowledging this truth: **Compatibility isn't convenience. Chemistry isn't commitment. Love isn't luck. It's intentional.**

Jeremy Sanford

Let's talk about it.

Dating vs. Courtship

Before we dive into why love can feel so elusive, let's start with the basics. Dating and courtship are *not* the same thing.

Dating is casual communication. There's little commitment—just two people getting to know each other. It's not a job interview or a vow of allegiance. It's conversation, curiosity, and the early discovery phase.

Ladies, when a man asks for your number, he's not proposing. He's inviting you into a conversation. So don't overthink it. Give him a chance if he seems kind and decent. And gentlemen, don't turn this season into a manipulative playground. If you're not feeling chemistry after the second date, move on with integrity. Let her be found by the man God *did* design for her.

Now, once you've dated and discovered that there's both **chemistry** and **compatibility**—that's when **courtship** begins. Courtship is intentional. It's exclusive. It's when you say, "I see something in you that makes me consider forever."

This is where faith, family, mentors, and prayer become more important than ever. If you want a love story that's not just sweet, but sustainable, you must seek wisdom.

Chemistry and Compatibility

Compatibility and chemistry are mostly ignored by dating advice because they're things that can't be faked or changed.

MARK MANSON

Chemistry is that magnetic pull, the butterflies, the ease of conversation. It's that moment you talk all night and can't wait to talk again.

When I first met Zaria, there was no awkward pause, no forced jokes—just flow. A first conversation that felt like reconnecting with a best friend. That's chemistry.

But chemistry alone isn't enough.

Compatibility is about alignment—lifestyle, beliefs, long-term vision. A woman who tithes faithfully, prays daily, and wants to raise her kids in church might hit it off with a man who's moral but sees Christianity as a "optional." Their chemistry is real—but their spiritual priorities pull them in opposite directions.

The goal is to have both. Chemistry without compatibility is short-lived fun. Compatibility without chemistry is a solid but dry friendship. But when you find both? That's the gold standard.

Biological Clocks & Timing Tensions

Let's talk about timing—because it's often one of the most misunderstood and mismatched parts of dating.

Women, understandably, tend to keep a close eye on the clock. The biological one. The societal one. The "I want to be a mom before 35" one. And pressure often comes from family too. Mothers and grandmothers—hear me with love: **please don't add more pressure.** Your daughter is already carrying it.

Men, on the other hand, are usually in no rush. A guy can be 35 and still feel like marriage is five years away. It's not because they don't want love—it's that they often feel like they need to "arrive" first.

But sometimes, those clocks align. And other times? They don't. That's where wisdom comes in.

I've seen it all:

- The woman who waits five years only to realize the man she loved never intended to marry her.
- The man who's ready but falls in love with a woman still chasing a degree, a promotion, or her own emotional healing.
- And even in my own story, I faced it with Zaria.

When we met, I was 27—two bachelor's degrees, a Master's, and ready to propose. Zaria was 22 and just finishing her undergrad. We were at different life stages. On our first official date in New Jersey—after lunch, the aquarium, and a walk in the park—we sat in a small pizza shop and talked timelines.

I would be ready for marriage in 2-3 years. She was not yet ready and needed much more time to complete her degrees.

We didn't have a heated debate. We didn't issue ultimatums. We acknowledged the tension—and agreed to keep learning each other.

Long story short: we made it work. Timing didn't divide us; communication united us.

Dating Protocols That Protect the Future

Now that you understand timing, chemistry, and compatibility, here are a few protocols to guide you through dating and courtship:

1. **Take your time**
   Don't rush commitment. Learn each other. Explore their family, their story, their values.

2. **Communicate your feelings**
   Don't play games. If you see long-term potential, speak it.

3. **Seek wise counsel**
   Pastors, mentors, parents—they see what love often overlooks. Use their insight.

4. **Evaluate both chemistry and compatibility**
   Passion is powerful, but shared values and vision are essential.

5. **Look at long-term potential**
   Maybe they're not ready now. But are they *becoming* someone who will be ready soon?

6. **Don't skip courtship**
   Casual dating is not enough to evaluate marriage potential. Move into a season of exclusivity and prayer.

7. **Get pre-marital counseling**
   You don't know what you don't know. Humble yourself and get equipped.

8. **Center the proposal and wedding on Christ**
   Don't major in the party and minor in the covenant.

Zaria's Dad and the Proposal Process

Fellas, if she has a father in her life—call him. Don't text. Don't DM. Ask for his blessing. Honor his role.

I called Zaria's father a couple weeks ago. He was accross the country, so it had to be a phone call. I opened with gratitude—thanked him and his wife for the amazing daughter they raised. I told him I loved her and wanted his blessing.

He said yes—with honor and joy. Then he gave me wisdom about how to keep her smiling. (Fathers know things. Listen.)

I didn't get just permission. I got insight. And that, my friends, is invaluable.

The Supply & Demand Myth

Let's address something else I hear all the time:

"There are no good men left."

False.

What's true is that in many social spaces—especially churches and campuses—women outnumber men. So yes, the competition feels fierce. But that doesn't mean quality men don't exist.

You may just need to position yourself differently. If you're a woman of value, make sure that your *preparation* matches your *expectation*.

Get your degree. Heal. Refine your communication. Strengthen your faith. Care for your body. Set yourself apart. Don't wait for him to arrive—be ready when he does.

And for the men—do the same. You want a strong woman of faith and character? Then *become* the man who attracts and deserves that kind of partner.

Don't just chase love. *Prepare for it.*

What About Expectations?

Let's be real. Sometimes women's expectations are sky-high. Sometimes men's expectations are non-existent.

Women might pass up a great man because he doesn't make six figures *yet*. Men might overlook a beautiful soul because she doesn't look like a social media model.

There has to be balance. Look for **potential, not perfection.** Look for **purpose over packaging.** Look beyond the present and ask: *Who could this person become if loved well?*

Also, **don't let single friends give relationship advice that doesn't match their own success.** Everyone has opinions, but few have fruit. Take advice from people who are where you want to go.

Final Thoughts: Becoming a Match

We often think love is about *finding* the perfect match.

But as Lysa TerKeurst said so beautifully, **great love is about *choosing* to be a match.** It's about working through your differences, aligning your timelines, navigating conflict with grace, and building a future together—*on purpose.*

Zaria and I didn't start with everything perfectly aligned. We had to work through timelines, expectations, and even some disagreements about the pace of our journey.

But we chose to grow together.

You can too.

Scriptural Reflection

"He who finds a wife finds a good thing and obtains favor from the Lord."

—Proverbs 18:22 (ESV)

This verse is often quoted, but let's not overlook its weight. A "wife" here is not just a woman—it's a woman who is *ready*. Prepared. Positioned. Walking in purpose.

And the man? He's not just any guy. He's a **finder**. Intentional. Decisive. Faith-filled.

Finding the right match isn't about waiting for fate. It's about aligning yourself with purpose, seeking God's voice, and being willing to grow together even when the timing doesn't look perfect.

Love doesn't have to be flawless to be faithful.
You may not start as a perfect match, but with God, you can *become* one.

That's a love worth waiting for.

And that's a love worth choosing—again and again.

CHAPTER

19

The Single Person's Anthem

It takes nothing to join the crowd.
It takes everything to stand alone

HANS F. HANSON
Retired professional football player and fashion advisor

Alright, alright—enough about how to get a woman or a man. This chapter is not a dating how-to or a "ten steps to bae" survival guide. This is your standing ovation moment, your soul's encore, your time to shine.

Let's raise a toast—Hawaiian Punch in hand—to every single soul who has chosen joy over despair, purpose over pity, and movement over misery. You're not waiting in a line to get picked. You are walking purposefully in the lane God already paved for you.

Let's be real: our culture glorifies romantic pairings. Power couples get the praise, engagement photos get the likes, and Hallmark movies get the tears. But I want to shine the spotlight on you—the single person doing extraordinary things on your own terms. This chapter is your anthem.

And if you're going to live it well, I suggest you live it like a Hall of Famer.

Take Kobe Bryant, for example. When the Lakers retired his jersey, they didn't retire one number—they retired *two*. #8 and #24. Each number represented a decade of dominance, a chapter of greatness. His stats in both jerseys were good enough for the Hall of Fame. Not once. Twice.

That's how I want you to think about your life. Your *single season* should be so rich, so productive, so purpose-driven, that even if marriage never came, it would be enough to earn eternal applause. But if marriage *does* come, let your single stats be so good they demand a banner in the rafters of your life.

At the beginning of writing this book, I was single. I didn't have anyone to call my own. I didn't know what she'd look like. Didn't know her name. But I had hope. I had faith that God wasn't teasing me—He was training me. I was learning to wait with purpose.

And in due time, I met Zaria. (Soon to be Zaria Sanford.)

But before I found her, I had to find *me*. And that's what this chapter is about. It's about the journey of becoming, of building, of blossoming in your single season.

This chapter is your game plan.

Travel Often, Travel Far

Don't just exist—*explore*. One of the greatest advantages of being single is the freedom to move. To pack your bags and chase new experiences. To discover who you are when you're far from what's familiar.

Married life brings joy, but it also brings logistical planning. You can't always hop on a plane or take a spontaneous road trip. That's why you should travel now—while your calendar only requires *your* approval.

During my single years, I made it my mission to see the country. Alabama, California, Colorado, Georgia, New York, Tennessee—the list goes on. Each place stretched my worldview and shattered my excuses. It reminded me that life is meant to be *lived*, not just endured.

Traveling lifts the fog of comparison. You realize that you don't need a partner to be joyful, to be inspired, to be fulfilled. In fact, some married people would pay good money to relive the independence you currently have. So don't squander it. Savor it.

> "Not that I speak in respect of want: for I have learned, in whatsoever state I am, therewith to be content."
> —Philippians 4:11, KJV

Invest in Your Physical Fitness

You only get one body. Honor it.

Marriage is beautiful, but it shifts priorities. Kids, careers, and calendar chaos will tug at your time. So, while you're single, set a fitness foundation that will carry you into the next season.

Don't wait until you "need" to lose weight. Build a proactive lifestyle now. Workout. Hydrate. Choose foods that give life instead of draining it. You don't have to become a gym rat—just become consistent.

Here are some tried and true basics:

- Water is your friend. Drink a lot.
- Choose baked over fried.
- Don't make soda your lifeline.
- Eat your greens. Your body will thank you.
- Move your body at least 3–4 times a week.

- Elevate your heart rate. Sweat a little. Or a lot.
- Rest between reps, but not for too long.
- Stay consistent.

A fit body supports a sound mind. And yes, it gives your future spouse something to admire. But more importantly, it gives *you* the energy to walk in purpose without burnout.

Save to Prosper

Don't just work for money—make your money work for your *future*.

Debt is one of the leading causes of divorce. Don't carry financial baggage into your next chapter. Pay off your debt. Start budgeting. Delay unnecessary spending. Build the discipline of financial stewardship.

I chose to create a personal budget. It changed everything. I tracked every dollar. I tithed consistently. I minimized waste. I saved nearly $20,000 during my single years—not because I was rich, but because I was *focused*.

Whether your goal is a home, a business, or simply peace of mind—start saving now. Here's a quick reminder:

- Make a monthly budget.
- Cut impulse spending.
- Tithe with intention (Malachi 3:10).
- Start an emergency fund ($1,000 minimum).
- Avoid overdraft fees like they're the plague.

> *"The plans of the diligent lead surely to abundance and advantage,*
> *But everyone who acts in haste comes surely to poverty."*
>
> —Proverbs 21:5, AMP

Learn to Cook

Your wallet and your waistline will both thank you.

Cooking is not just a skill. It's an act of self-care. It gives you control over what goes into your body and saves you thousands every year.

Here's a little math: Spending $25 a day on meals = $9,000/year. Cooking at home for $100/week = $5,000/year. That's a $4,000 difference—money that could fund your savings, investment, or vacation goals.

Learning to cook also prepares you to serve someone else. Imagine your future spouse walking in from a long day and you've got their favorite meal ready. That's not old-fashioned. That's love in action.

Ladies, fellas—yes, even *you*—learn a few staple meals now. Take a class. Watch YouTube. Call your grandma. Whatever it takes. Your future self (and future spouse) will thank you.

Help Someone Else

You weren't created to live for yourself.

Singleness is a powerful opportunity to give. To volunteer. To mentor. To pour into others without waiting for a ring to give you purpose.

I've served at homeless shelters. I've tutored students. I've invested time into church ministry. And every time, I walked away more grateful, more fulfilled, and more aligned with my divine assignment.

Impact isn't just for when you're married. It's for *now*.

> *"And whatsoever ye do, do it heartily, as
> to the Lord, and not unto men."*
> —Colossians 3:23, KJV

Final Thoughts: Singleness Is a Masterpiece in Progress

I want to remind you—singleness is not a curse. It's not a waiting room. It's a masterpiece in progress.

Some people look at art and see chaos—colors smeared on canvas, shapes without meaning. But to the trained eye, it's beautiful. Strategic. Sacred.

Your single life is that canvas. And God is still painting.

So, walk tall. Live boldly. Say yes to purpose. Say no to pity. You are not missing out. You are *leveling up*.

Scriptural Reflection

> *"To everything there is a season, and a time
> to every purpose under the heaven."*
> —Ecclesiastes 3:1 (KJV)

This is your season. Don't wish it away. Don't envy another's chapter. Embrace your now with all your heart.

Your time for love may be coming. But your time for purpose is *already here*.

Live it. Own it. Honor it.

Because when Zaria—or whoever God's chosen one is for you—comes along, they should find you in your purpose, not hiding from it.

And when that day comes, you'll be able to say with joy and peace:

"I didn't just wait. I *worked*. I didn't just dream. I *became*."

Now that, my friend, is how you enter the Hall of Fame.

CHAPTER

20

Ageless Love

You can fall in love at any age whether it's 80 or 5

JUSTIN BIEBER
Canadian Singer and songwriter

Romance is possible between two people at any age!
I love feeling young and acting young as I age

KIM ALEXIS
American model and actress

Who doesn't want to be loved?

From the tiniest toddler to the wisest senior, love is a pursuit woven into every season of life. I've seen people lose their spouses of 40+ years and still, with wrinkled hands and silver hair, search once more for companionship. Not because they're lonely—but because love never grows old. That's what I call **ageless love**.

Ageless love is a flame that refuses to die. It transcends birthdays, bodies, and years. It's the kind of love that keeps a glimmer in your eye even when your bones ache. The type of connection where even in your 80s, you laugh like it's your first date.

That's the kind of love I want. And that's the kind of love I believe we all deserve.

Now, let me share a principle that changed everything for me during my relationship with Zaria: **a soft answer.**

Men—hear me clearly. This one is gold. You can end 90% of arguments before they begin if you simply respond with softness. That's right, not strength. *Softness.*

> *"A soft answer turneth away wrath: but grievous words stir up anger."*
> —Proverbs 15:1 (KJV)

Zaria and I are both strong-willed, passionate people. Early on, disagreements could turn into debates. And debates could spark into fires. Until I realized—I wasn't fighting *her*, I was fighting *with* her. That's a dangerous game.

So, I made a shift. I lowered my tone. I listened. I gave a soft answer. And almost immediately, the flames cooled. Arguments lost their fuel. Reconciliation happened faster. And peace settled in.

When you respond in love, with humility, your relationship doesn't lose—it *wins*. Love doesn't demand victory. It seeks resolution.

Trust me. If you want to keep the fire of ageless love burning, stop throwing gasoline. Start responding with grace.

Love is Essential

Love is our essential nutrient. Without it, life has little meaning. It's the best thing we have to give and the most valuable thing we receive.

CHERYL STRAYED

We are wired to crave love. From birth to our final breath, we want to be seen, valued, and embraced.

This longing doesn't fade. It matures. As children, it starts with our parents. As teens, it shifts to crushes and curiosity. As adults, it becomes about deep connection, shared purpose, and emotional safety.

Even when love wounds us, we return to it. Why? Because love is not a luxury. It's a necessity.

Enter Abraham Maslow, the psychologist who gave us the **Hierarchy of Needs**. His chart lists what motivates human behavior—starting with air, food, and water. But not far up that pyramid is love and belonging.

Maslow knew what Scripture already affirmed:

> "And now abideth faith, hope, charity, these three; but the greatest of these is charity."
> —1 Corinthians 13:13, KJV

Charity here means love. Love remains the greatest force we will ever know.

Love can come from family, friends, and romantic partners. And while each form looks different, the impact is the same—it fills the human heart.

Whether through a friend who stays through every storm or a spouse who sees you fully and loves you anyway, love is essential. It's not optional. It's oxygen for the soul.

We Need Love Like We Need Air

Pleasure is, after all, a luxury. It's love that's essential.

JOHN DUFRESNE

Once you feel safe and secure in life, love becomes the next hunger to satisfy.

Why are dating apps booming? Why do people binge romance movies? Why do even the toughest men crack when they hold their baby for the first time?

Because we *need* love. Badly.

Family often gives us our first taste of it. Then friendships grow the concept. But romantic love? That's the wild card. The beautiful, risky, vulnerable, exhilarating expression that gets under your skin and into your dreams.

That longing led me to write this book. I was whole in many areas—but that one was missing. So, I wrote. I prayed. I grew. And then, I met Zaria.

You might not have seen your person yet. But believe this: **what you want is also looking for you.**

Keep becoming. Keep showing up. Keep loving where you are, and love will meet you there.

Try Love Again

Some of us have scars. Real ones. From betrayal. From divorce. From disappointments that shattered our expectations and hardened our hearts.

But let me offer you hope: You *can* love again.

Will it take time? Yes. Will it take courage? Absolutely. But your story isn't over. The next chapter may be the sweetest one yet.

Instead of dwelling on what you lost, focus on what you *learned*. Every painful experience can sharpen your discernment and refine your desires.

You're not starting over. You're starting wiser.

God doesn't waste heartbreak. He uses it to prepare you for better. And I promise, better is coming.

> *"And I will restore to you the years that the locust hath eaten..."*
> —Joel 2:25 (KJV)

God can give you back *time*. He can redeem the story. He can rebuild the joy.

So, dare to believe again. Open your heart again. Smile again. Hope again. And yes—*love again.*

Scriptural Reflection

> *"Beloved, let us love one another: for love is of God; and every one that loveth is born of God, and knoweth God."*
> —1 John 4:7 (KJV)

Love isn't just a feeling. It's divine DNA. It's the fingerprint of heaven placed on every human heart.

Whether you're in your 20s or your 80s, God has more love for you to give and receive. He's not finished. He's just getting started.

So, open your hands, open your heart, and open your life to the greatest gift of all.

Because when love leads the way, joy follows close behind.

Love again. Believe again. And prepare—because your next chapter might be your best one yet.

CHAPTER

21

When Destinies Collide

What is meant to be will always find a way

TRISHA YEARWOOD
Country music singer, author, actress, and chef

A person often meets his destiny on the road that he took to avoid it

JEAN DE LA FONTAINE
French fabulist and world-renowned poet

There's something magical about divine intersections—when purpose meets providence, when preparation meets promise, when two destinies, previously on separate tracks, collide with grace and intentionality. There are few things as sacred and stunning as watching love unfold in God's timing. Regardless of where you're from or how stoic your exterior may be, love—real love—has a way of breaking down every wall.

We're all drawn to good love stories. They inspire us, challenge us, and breathe hope into our waiting seasons. Not because love is always easy or perfect, but because when it's right, it's *holy*. In this chapter, I'll share the stories of three remarkable couples who found each other and chose to build something that would stand the test of time. Their testimonies are proof that when God authors the story, it always reads better than fiction.

The A-Team

Success in marriage is more than finding the right person; it is being the right person.

ROBERT BROWNING

Aaron and Allison didn't just fall in love—they *built* a love. Hailing from Indianapolis, Indiana, their story has always stood out to me because of how grounded and God-honoring it is. Over the years, I've watched their union blossom—not just in beauty, but in strength, maturity, and clarity. They've not only built a life together; they've built a legacy.

When asked to title the book that best describes their marriage, Allison responded with the profound: **"Just Keep Pressing."** That's not just a phrase—it's a lifestyle. She said, "Behind every good relationship is a story of prayer, perseverance, and praise." Marriage isn't magic—it's ministry. It's two people deciding, day in and day out, to press forward, even through the storm and rain. She added, "When God blesses you, don't ever forget the prayers it took to get there."

Aaron, always insightful, suggested a few titles: **"The Real," "The Good, the Bad, and the Ugly,"** and **"Marriage Life: What It Really Is."** His words reminded me of a truth we often overlook: marriage isn't just romance—it's reality. And reality requires both people to come fully present, willing to grow, give, forgive, and sometimes even fail forward.

Before marriage, they had their share of challenges. Like many couples, they walked through bumps in the road, learning that love alone isn't enough—perspective is crucial. Social media gives people a curated highlight reel of relationships, but real marriage is lived in the behind-the-scenes footage—where compromise, communication, and Christ make the difference.

Their story began in the most unassuming way: over a stick of gum. Aaron, working a media event with over 100,000 attendees, was finishing his lunch when Allison, who had recognized him from Facebook, casually asked for a piece of gum. That moment became a doorway. A few messages later on Facebook—and destiny was set in motion.

What struck Allison about Aaron wasn't what she was looking for—it was what she didn't know she needed. His professionalism, focus, and intentionality captivated her. "God gave me something I wasn't even praying for," she admitted. Aaron, on the other hand, admired her groundedness, her upbringing, and most of all, her unwavering support.

One of the secrets to their continued success? Intentional one-on-one time. Before children, they were goal-oriented—saving money, traveling, purchasing their home. When kids entered the picture, they didn't let busyness erode their bond. They remained intentional. Date nights. Vacations without the kids. And small, daily choices to pursue one another.

What advice would they give to those preparing for marriage?

Aaron put it plainly: "Pray. Make sure it's God's will. And don't expect to change someone. Who they are when you're dating is often magnified in marriage." He also emphasized practical preparation: have a job, transportation, and a stable place to live. "Love won't pay rent," he said, "and flat tires don't wait on faith."

Allison added, "Appreciate the season you're in. Don't rush. Don't romanticize what you see online. Marriage is not a fairytale—it's a divine assignment."

Their pillars are prayer, communication, and effort. Allison summed it up best: "I can't just pray for Aaron to change—I have to ask God to change me first."

Jeremy Sanford

Committed to the End

There is no abiding success without commitment.

TONY ROBBINS

Some love stories are subtle symphonies that crescendo over decades. Melba and Ricky Bolden have been married for 30 years. Their relationship is not only a testament to God's faithfulness, but also a blueprint for endurance in a generation that often treats marriage as disposable.

When asked what book would describe their marriage, Melba answered without hesitation: **"Committed to the End."** And Ricky? He simply said, "I concur."

Their beginning was humble and sweet. At just 14, Ricky was leading summer community service projects at his grandfather's church. Melba was one of the younger kids on his team. She was feisty, independent, and—ironically—resistant to his instructions. Yet something about her spirit stuck with him. "One day," he said, "I thought to myself, 'She's going to make someone an amazing wife.' I had no idea that someone would be me."

Years later, Ricky gave his life to Christ and began serving in the church. Soon after, Melba also surrendered her life to the Lord. The day after Melba got saved, Ricky called her. And just like that, what God had written in the background began to unfold in the foreground.

Dating wasn't without its difficulties. There was one significant breakup, sparked by misaligned timelines. Ricky was ready to marry; Melba wasn't. She was 23 and had always imagined marrying at 25. Though their separation was painful, it was necessary. It brought clarity. And two weeks after Melba turned 25, they were husband and wife.

Their story is filled with practical wisdom. From setting early bedtimes for their children to carving out time for "James Bond movie nights," they understood the value of prioritizing one another—even in the thick of parenting.

Their advice? Melba urges young people to *be whole before getting married.* "Don't marry to be completed. Marry to complement." Ricky echoed the need for openness: "Ask the real questions. Do you want kids? What's your financial mindset? Don't assume. Ask."

The glue that held them together? A serious view of commitment. Ricky said, "I took my vows seriously. I meant them. 'Til death' wasn't a poetic phrase—it was a promise." He also emphasized shared responsibility and recognizing each other's strengths: "If one of us is better with money, they handle the finances. Marriage isn't about proving points—it's about playing to your strengths."

Melba offered this powerful insight: "Within the church, we sometimes rely on the Holy Ghost as the *only* filter for compatibility. But the Holy Ghost doesn't pay the bills. Practical alignment matters too."

Ricky shared a profound story—one that speaks to the power of perspective. A man once complained that his wife made them late for church because she was slow getting the kids ready. Ricky gently reminded him: "She got herself and three children ready—while you got yourself dressed and waited. If you keep living like that, you'll wear her out." That lesson stayed with the man—and with me.

Marriage is Beautiful

A successful marriage requires falling in love many times, always with the same person.

MIGNON MCLAUGHLIN

The final couple I want to honor is my own foundation: my parents—James and Hazel Sanford. For over three decades, they've modeled not only marriage but ministry. What I admire most is how their love never needed a stage to be powerful. It simply *was*. Faithful. Consistent. Humble. Steady.

When asked to describe their marriage in a book title, they gave poetic answers:

James – *Let's Do It Again*
Hazel – *Once Upon a Time*

They met at a church convention in Houston. James noticed Hazel's elegance—her dress, her posture, her presence. Hazel admired James' poise and the fact that he traveled with his mother and sister—a detail that quietly revealed his character.

Hazel described James as calm, thoughtful, and disciplined. He handled pressure well and exuded the kind of quiet strength that made her feel safe. James loved Hazel's ambition, drive, and warmth. Their differences didn't divide them—they sharpened one another.

Their dating journey had its share of misunderstandings, but no breakups. Both agree: frequent breakups during courtship should raise red flags. Hazel noted, "How someone handles disagreement in dating is often a preview of how they'll handle conflict in marriage."

Their insight into 1-on-1 time was powerful. James said, "It's not just about spending time—it's about eliminating distractions. Turn off the phones. Protect the sacred." Hazel added, "When the kids were young, we made bedtime a priority. Our time together mattered—not just for our marriage but for their emotional well-being."

Their greatest advice to aspiring couples? Ask every question. Know who you're marrying. Don't assume—*investigate.* And when you commit, do so with a spirit that says: *failure is not an option.*

Hazel's final piece of wisdom was simple yet profound: "Forgive quickly. Carry grace like it's oxygen. It's the only way love survives the weight of life."

Scriptural Reflection

"Two are better than one, because they have a good reward for their labor. For if they fall, one will lift up his companion."

—Ecclesiastes 4:9–10 (NKJV)

Each of these couples proves what Scripture has always affirmed—*love is strongest when it lifts.* Marriage isn't just about happiness. It's about holiness. It's not about convenience—it's about covenant. The journey will test you, stretch you, and mold you. But when God is at the center, your marriage becomes more than a partnership—it becomes a purpose-driven union that blesses everyone it touches.

To those still waiting: don't lose hope. What's meant for you will never miss you. When destinies collide under the hand of God, beauty is inevitable. And if He's writing your story, trust me—you're in for a masterpiece.

CHAPTER

22

I Thought I Did, But I Don't

*Sometimes the hardest decisions in life are
the ones that define our destiny.*

UNKNOWN

The Proposal

When love is led by God, it rarely shows up the way you imagined—but always arrives right on time.

As I look back over this journey—one filled with faith, hope, reflection, and growth—what started as a desire to understand love ended with me discovering the person God had been preparing all along. Her name is Zaria, and the moment our paths crossed, everything in me knew: this is the one I prayed for before I knew how to pray for her.

The road to Zaria wasn't paved with perfection. There were challenges, misunderstandings, and moments of honest questioning. But if there's one truth I've learned, it's this: true love doesn't avoid the hard conversations—it survives them. In fact, it's often forged through them. Even the most God-ordained relationships will face adversity. But when love is real, it isn't frightened by the fire—it's refined by it.

When the time came to propose, I had saved, prayed, and planned down to the detail. But the night before the ring was purchased, we had a disagreement. It nearly derailed what was supposed to be a celebration. I questioned the timing. I questioned the day. But in the stillness of that moment, I thought to myself: Love is not about perfection—it's about persistence. And just like that, with one unexpected "I love you" from Zaria, clarity returned. Love doesn't require the absence of tension—it simply requires the presence of commitment.

The proposal was unforgettable. Family and friends gathered. Music played. A custom-written song called "Hey Zaria" filled the room. I knelt, ring in hand, and asked the most important question of my life. With tears in her eyes, she said, "Yes."

That "yes" wasn't to a perfect man or a perfect life—but to a future built on faith, friendship, and a relentless commitment to keep choosing each other every single day.

The Realization

Life has a way of testing our resolve in ways we never expect. Just when I thought I had found the love of my life, I came to the sobering realization that I hadn't. Through much prayer, reflection, and divine clarity, I made one of the hardest decisions of my life: I called off the wedding.

This wasn't a decision made in fear or haste. It was revelation—God pulling back the curtain and showing me things I had either missed or refused to see. This was more than red flags; it was divine disalignment.

When someone shows you who they are, believe them the first time.

MAYA ANGELOU

The specifics aren't what matter here. What matters is that when God tells you it's time to release something—or someone—you don't hold on out of sentiment. The proposal video had over 30,000 views. Deposits were made. The wedding dress was picked out. But when peace leaves, pay attention.

She was shocked. Hurt. She asked the questions anyone would ask: Why now? Could we fix it? I answered with as much grace and honesty as I could. But this wasn't about fixing. This was about freedom. For both of us.

Honesty is a very expensive gift. Don't expect it from cheap people.
WARREN BUFFETT

When the call ended, I knew a chapter had closed. I also knew that many wouldn't understand. Some wouldn't approve. And a few would even mock it. But I'd rather endure temporary pain than walk into a permanent mistake.

The Fallout

The months that followed felt like navigating fog. Ending a deep relationship, especially one rooted in friendship, is a grief unlike any other. You're not just mourning the person; you're mourning the life you imagined together.

People said, "You'll find someone else," or "Everything happens for a reason." But those words, though well-meaning, felt hollow. I didn't want a replacement. I wanted rest.

Oddly, being single again drew attention. Suddenly, DMs were full. Friends were matchmaking. People were calculating my availability. Some saw me as a risk. Others saw me as a catch. I saw myself as a man learning to breathe again.

I remember preaching just weeks after the breakup. I walked off stage, and a friend immediately pulled out his phone: "Bro, I have someone you need to meet." I smiled politely, but I wasn't ready. Not yet. Maybe not for a long time.

To the One Who's Waiting

If you're in a serious relationship or engaged, hear me clearly:

Until you say "I do," you have every right to pause.

Not out of fear, but out of wisdom.

Marriage is not a lease agreement. It's a lifelong covenant. Too many walk down the aisle to please family, avoid shame, or prove a point. And too many regret it later.

If you have doubts, don't ignore them. If you feel tension, don't silence it. If God speaks, *obey*.

> *Marriage is not about finding someone you can live with,*
> *it's about finding someone you can't live without.*
> UNKNOWN

Ladies, if he lacks integrity while you're dating, marriage won't fix that. The altar doesn't alter character.

Gentlemen, don't ignore your peace just to fulfill a timeline. Better to endure whispers now than to live in silence later.

Alignment Over Attraction

During my single years, I read dozens of books on marriage preparation. But many of them skipped over one essential principle:

Love isn't enough. Alignment is essential.

I admired the book *The Wait* by DeVon Franklin and Meagan Good. But even their story—rooted in sexual purity—ended in divorce. It taught me this: abstaining from sex doesn't guarantee alignment. Vision, purpose, values, and spiritual trajectory must all be on the same path.

The Bible asks: *"Can two walk together, except they be agreed?"* (Amos 3:3)

Compatibility isn't just about shared interests; it's about shared calling.

Ask better questions:

- What are you building?
- Where are you going?
- What do you value at your core?

Romance can blind. So can religion. But purpose brings clarity. If you know what God has called you to build, you won't waste time with someone who isn't meant to help you build it.

Owning the Mistake

Should I have known sooner? Probably. Should I have waited before proposing? Maybe. Should I have spared us both the pain? Possibly.

But here's what I do know: *I learned.* And I'm sharing it so someone else doesn't have to learn the hard way.

Because the deeper the entanglement, the harder the exit. And most won't leave once money, memories, and emotions are all invested. But staying out of fear is a prison. And marriage should never feel like confinement.

Jeremy Sanford

> *There is no more lovely, friendly, and charming relationship, communion, or company than a good marriage.*
>
> MARTIN LUTHER

Good marriage is possible. Kingdom partnership is real. But it requires clarity before the covenant.

I walked away, not because I stopped loving her, but because I started loving obedience more.

I chose God's will over good intentions. And that decision saved both of us from a lifetime of trying to force something that was never designed to fit.

Now, with fresh clarity and deeper wisdom, I look ahead. And in the next chapter, I'll tell you how I met the woman I'm married to now—and how it all made sense.

Scriptural Reflection

> *"Trust in the Lord with all your heart and lean not on your own understanding; in all your ways submit to Him, and He will make your paths straight."*
>
> —Proverbs 3:5-6 (NIV)

There will be moments when your understanding fails you—when your emotions cloud your discernment. But if you trust God with the blueprint, He will redirect your steps. Let obedience guide you, not obligation.

Some doors are closed by God not to punish you, but to protect you.

Sometimes walking away isn't giving up—it's growing up.

Turn the page.

CHAPTER

23

The Flight That Changed My Life

Everything you want is on the other side of fear.

JACK CANFIELD

The winter of 2019 marked the end of one chapter and the trembling start of another. After calling off my wedding—a decision rooted in clarity but birthed through anguish—I found myself suspended in a space between heartbreak and healing. I had said goodbye to what I thought was forever and stood at the edge of "what's next?" with nothing but faith in my pocket.

For months, I let silence do the talking. No dating. No searching. Just stillness. But when you're wired for connection—when you know you've been called to build not just *a life*, but *a legacy* with someone—eventually, the heart begins to whisper, *"It's time."*

And so, nervously, I stepped back into the world of dating. It felt foreign. Mechanical. Exhausting. Like trying to write a new book using the ashes of the last one.

Dating After Detour

Over the next year, I met three incredible women. Each brought light in different ways—kind, ambitious, beautiful inside and out. We laughed, shared stories, exchanged dreams. But something within me never fully clicked.

They were good. Just not *her*.

I don't mean that in a fairytale sense. I simply mean there was no spiritual lock-and-key. No deep resonance. No confirmation from Heaven that this was the woman whose hand I was meant to hold through storm and success.

By the end of 2020, I had all but surrendered to the timeline of God. "If it takes years, Lord, so be it," I whispered one night. But still, deep down, I hoped it wouldn't.

Then, as divine stories often begin—not in a spotlight, but in the mundane—I found myself scrolling on social media when a photo caught my eye.

Her name was **LaTresha Reed**.

More Than a Profile

I've learned that social media is both a window and a mirror—what we see in others often reflects what we long for in ourselves. But after seeing too many curated personas crumble under reality, I'd become cautious.

Still, something about her made me pause. It wasn't just her beauty—it was her poise. Her presence radiated through the pixels.

Then I noticed a familiar name: **Bernard Gladney**. A man of integrity. A friend. A brother in the faith. If she was in *his* circle, I knew there was depth behind the image.

I called Bernard immediately. "Tell me about LaTresha."

"She's incredible," he said. "Sharp. Graceful. Her father's a pastor. And Jeremy... she's not easy to get."

That last part? It hooked me.

Challenge accepted.

(Quick note to the ladies: the pursuit is not just romantic—it's spiritual. There's something sacred about being pursued by a man on assignment. Don't cheapen your value by being too available too soon.)

A few days later, Bernard called me back.

"She's single. If you come to Michigan, my wife and I will make the introduction."

It just so happened I had an unused flight credit. Destiny had my full attention.

Michigan

That Friday night, I walked into a church service where LaTresha was moderating. From the moment I saw her, I knew this wasn't going to be just another introduction.

She was poised, articulate, composed. There was something regal about her—like she had nothing to prove, and yet, her presence did all the speaking for her.

After service, my friends got distracted in conversation. I wasn't about to miss my moment.

I approached her directly.

"Praise the Lord. My name is Jeremy. How are you?"

She smiled. "I'm well, thank you."

It was brief. But the tone was set. Later, our mutual friends arranged a double date.

The Date That Shifted My Soul

We met at *The Sauce*, a quaint Italian spot in downtown Flint, Michigan. The lighting was dim. The music low. When she arrived—fashionably late—every eye in the room paused.

She wore a fitted black skirt and a sleek blouse. Sophistication in motion.

Our friends did most of the talking at dinner. I mostly observed her—the way she listened, the grace in her silence. I wanted time alone.

So, as the night ended, I offered, "May I walk you to your car?"

She agreed.

As we neared her vehicle, I took the risk: "Can I take you out to dinner tomorrow?"

She hesitated, "Are you sure you won't be too tired after preaching?"

Her understanding impressed me. "I'll have energy for this," I replied.

She smiled. "Alright."

The next day, I preached in Port Huron, then texted her to confirm.

She asked again if I was sure I wasn't too tired. I wasn't. I was expectant.

We met at *Black Rock*, a unique steakhouse where you cook your meat on a volcanic stone. I arrived early. She arrived… *glorious*.

Long overcoat. Black leather skirt. Five-inch boots. Betsey Johnson glasses. Curled hair. And a confidence that made the room tilt.

I was not ready.

We talked for five straight hours. Faith. Business. Legacy. Our conversation moved like jazz—unplanned but perfectly in sync.

When the restaurant staff started stacking chairs, we hadn't even noticed. We were lost in time.

As I walked her to her car, I asked, "Can I give you a hug?"

She nodded.

That hug ended the search. I knew.

The Airport Revelation

The next morning, I sat at the airport, heart full and mind racing. I sent her a light text to keep the thread going.

Then my phone rang. It was my mother.

"Have you called her yet?" she asked.

"No. I was going to wait until tomorrow."

She didn't miss a beat.

"Don't wait. Call her now."

That's all I needed.

I called.

She was busy working on projects for her salon. But that call turned into hours. And from that day forward, not a single day passed without us speaking.

It wasn't forced. It flowed.

It didn't feel rushed. It felt *ready*.

Divine Confirmation

Days later, I wrote in the notes section of my phone: *"I believe this is my wife."*

I told no one. Not yet. But I prayed. I fasted. I asked God for clarity, not just confirmation.

After a few months, I called her father.

"I've been praying, sir. And I truly believe God is showing me that LaTresha is my future wife."

He paused.

"Jeremy, I think you need more time to observe her temperament."

At first, I bristled. I felt ready.

But now, I thank God for that pause.

Because in love—and in life—*timing* matters as much as *truth*.

I waited.

Months later, he invited me to breakfast at Bob Evans. We talked for over an hour. Then he looked at me with steady eyes and said:

"Yes. You may have my daughter's hand in marriage."

I smiled. "Thank you, sir."

Now, only one mission remained: plan a proposal that would stop time.

She had already changed my life. Now, I wanted to change her last name.

Scriptural Reflection

*"Delight yourself in the Lord, and He will
give you the desires of your heart."*
—Psalm 37:4 (ESV)

This chapter isn't about a lucky flight or perfect timing—it's about surrender.

It's about letting go of *your* timeline so you can walk into *God's* divine intersection.

The woman I met that day wasn't just an answer to prayer—she was a testament to what happens when you walk through heartbreak and *still* believe. When you let go of fear and choose to hope again. When you understand that just because something ends doesn't mean the story is over.

God doesn't tease His children. He doesn't tempt with counterfeits. When He delivers, it's complete. It's restorative. It's *exactly what you need, when you need it*.

But here's the secret: you don't find "the one" by chasing them.
You find them by becoming the kind of person who attracts what you're praying for.

So be faithful in the healing. Be present in the waiting. And never forget:

Sometimes, one flight—one moment of courage—can change everything.

CHAPTER

24

God Saved the Best for Last

The Lord is good to those who wait for Him, to the soul who seeks Him.

LAMENTATIONS 3:25

There are moments in life when God makes it abundantly clear: *This is what you were waiting for.*

The proposal wasn't just a milestone—it was the crescendo of a divine love story. After all the lessons, the heartbreak, and the waiting, I knew I couldn't propose to LaTresha with anything ordinary. She was anything but ordinary. She was grace, elegance, power, and prayer personified.

So, I planned a moment as unforgettable as the woman I had been blessed to love.

The Ring That Spoke Volumes

Let me be honest—this ring cost me a small fortune. But it wasn't about cost. It was about *commitment*. I had it custom-made, a radiant-cut diamond that caught the light in a way that said: *She is treasured.*

Fellas, hear me—don't buy a ring just to impress people. Buy a ring that reflects her style and your sincerity. When a man proposes, he's not just giving a piece of jewelry. He's placing his heart in her hands. My choice said: "She's not just loved—she's *honored*."

Setting the Stage

My plan was flawless. A violin. A candlelit dinner. A location so romantic it could've made the stars blush. The proposal was set for her next trip to Mississippi.

Now let me tell you—no instrument sets the tone quite like the violin. There's something in the way it sings. Each note is a whisper from the soul, and I wanted the soundtrack of our engagement to feel like a melody God Himself composed.

The night arrived. She thought we were headed to a fancy steakhouse. She wore a sleek black dress, red-bottom heels, and a glow that made my knees weak.

As we approached the clock tower at a scenic outdoor shopping area, my violinist messaged me—he was in place.

I took her hand. The cobblestones made her stumble slightly, and she held onto me tightly. We reached the tower.

"Look at that," I said, pointing upward.

She turned to look, confused. "What am I looking at?"

She turned back around—and there I was, on one knee.

Her hand flew to her mouth. Her eyes filled with tears.

My rehearsed speech? Gone.

What remained was the truth.

"LaTresha Rena Ruby Reed, will you marry me?"

Through tears and trembling, she whispered, "Yes."

A Night to Remember

The celebration began immediately. She FaceTimed her family, her smile as radiant as the diamond on her hand. We had dinner, but food was the least important part. That night was about the beginning of forever.

And just like that, we were engaged.

But love stories rarely unfold without twists.

The Unexpected Injury

Months before the wedding, I injured my Achilles during a basketball game. I hit the floor, pain shooting through me. My first thought wasn't the pain—it was *her*.

Would I walk down the aisle? Would I delay the wedding?

LaTresha's response? Pure grace.

She never flinched. Never made me feel like a burden. She became my greatest encourager. Through twice-a-week rehab, learning to walk again, and facing doubt, she stood firm.

We postponed the wedding by two months. Every step in therapy was taken with one goal in mind: *walk to my bride*.

And by the grace of God, I did.

A Wedding Made in Heaven

The day arrived. Hundreds gathered. Hundreds more watched online. The love in the room was tangible.

And then, she walked in.

But not just walked—she *sang*.

As she entered, escorted by her father, singing to me with a voice that melted every ounce of composure I had, I felt it: *God saved the best for last.*

Our Vows

My Vow:

LaTresha,

When I look at you, I see a symbol of God's faithfulness. Strength. Dignity. Grace. Perseverance. Before I met you, I prayed for you. And now, I stand before you, looking at the answer to every one of those prayers. You are my answered prayer.

I vow to love you all the days of my life. I vow to protect you—physically, emotionally, and spiritually. I pledge to be a faithful and prayerful husband and a devoted father. In the words of Jesus, I vow to never leave you nor forsake you.

I vow to apologize when I'm wrong. I promise to support you in every way possible because I want to see you achieve things you once thought were unimaginable.

There will be hard days. Storms will come. But I promise to weather them with you. We will endure because God's love always shines through. I love you, and I am yours forever.

Her Vow:

Jeremy,

My vows began long before you arrived. They started in my devotion to God—choosing to wait, choosing to trust, choosing to let Him mold me into the woman made just for you.

I stand here today in awe of God's faithfulness. His love for me is limitless, and now, I get to experience His love through you. You are a testament to the miracles of His love.

It was a miracle that we waited in this day and time. It was a miracle that you found me—hidden not because I was lost, but because the one I was made for would have to search in God to discover me.

You are that man. A man of God. A man of integrity. A man of vision.

So today, without hesitation, I vow to give you my greatest gift.

I vow to give you me.

A Love Worth Celebrating

The reception was electric. Food that made people dance in their seats. Laughter that echoed like worship. A room filled with love and legacy.

And when the night ended, it was only the beginning.

I married the woman of my dreams. The woman I loved before I ever met her. The one God hid for the right moment.

And now, with one final chapter left, I get to tell you what life looks like—not as a man waiting for love, but as a man walking in it every single day.

Scriptural Reflection

"He who finds a wife finds a good thing and obtains favor from the Lord."
—Proverbs 18:22 (NKJV)

What we often forget is that favor doesn't always come fast. It comes in God's time, to the one who's prepared to receive it.

God doesn't just give good gifts—He gives *perfectly timed* ones.

LaTresha wasn't late. She wasn't early. She was *right on time*.

God saved the best for last.

And if you've been waiting, wondering, praying—hold on.

Your final chapter is being written. Don't miss it.

The story isn't over—it's just getting started. The best part is waiting on the next page.

CHAPTER

25

Living the Dream I Prayed For

Unless the Lord builds the house, the builders labor in vain.

PSALM 127:1 (NIV)

I used to wonder what it would feel like to finally say, "I'm married." Not just because of the title or the ring, but because of what it meant: I found the one I waited for, prayed for, prepared for. Now, I wake up every day beside the woman I once only imagined. And let me tell you—marriage, when done God's way, is not just beautiful. It's *transformational*.

LaTresha and I are not perfect. But we're perfectly aligned in purpose, and that has made all the difference.

The Reality of Forever

Marriage is not a fairytale. It's not a series of Instagrammable moments or a reel of perfect dinners and romantic date nights. It's raw. It's real. It's a daily commitment to choose love, even when emotions fade. And while marriage doesn't fix everything, it *refines* everything.

There are moments when we misunderstand each other. Moments when silence fills the room longer than either of us would like. Moments when we have to relearn each other because growth changes us. But every challenge has been an invitation to love deeper, to listen harder, and to forgive faster.

The truth is, the good days far outweigh the tough ones. There are days we laugh over the smallest things until our stomachs hurt. Nights we fall asleep holding hands. Mornings when a simple "I'm proud of you" means more than a thousand compliments. That's the magic of covenant.

Marriage Isn't Just Living Together— It's Growing Together

Living with someone requires a new level of humility. Suddenly, your space, habits, and rhythms are intertwined with another person's. And as romantic as it sounds, it takes work. Communication becomes a discipline. Patience becomes a priority. Grace becomes a necessity.

We had to learn that marriage isn't about who's right—it's about what is right. It isn't about keeping score; it's about keeping peace. And that peace, I've found, doesn't come from having all the answers. It comes from knowing you're committed to *finding them together.*

I think back often to how long I waited. Twelve years of questions. Disappointments. Almosts. Heartbreaks. But when I look at LaTresha, I see why the wait was necessary. She wasn't just worth the wait—*she made the wait make sense.*

She is strong, thoughtful, graceful, and hilarious. Her smile lights up rooms, and her prayers cover our home. She is the calm to my storm, the answer to my asking, the love I believed in before I ever saw her face.

Choose Without a Plan B

One of the greatest decisions we made early on was to enter this covenant without a plan B. Divorce is not an escape route we entertain. That decision has shifted the way we show up for each other.

When you remove the option to leave, you lean into the work required to stay. We don't run from discomfort—we confront it. We don't retreat in silence—we reach for connection. Our commitment isn't fragile. It's fortified by our faith.

Marriage, at its best, is not about finding someone you can live with. It's about choosing someone you can't imagine living without. And every time I look at LaTresha, I know I'd choose her again and again. No hesitation. No doubt.

Learning in Love

We're learning how to be a team in the mundane and in the milestones. Whether it's planning our future, navigating finances, or deciding what's for dinner, we are learning to listen not just to each other's words, but to each other's hearts.

And honestly? I love it here.

I love the way we dance in the kitchen to songs only we understand. I love our spontaneous road trips. I love the way she says, "Let's pray about it" when I start to spiral. I love our shared dreams and the way our visions complement each other.

Love isn't just a feeling—it's a rhythm. And we're finding ours with every sunrise.

When You Marry Your Purpose Partner

Marriage gets sweeter when you marry someone who pulls purpose out of you. LaTresha challenges me, not just as a man, but as a visionary, a speaker, a leader, and a servant of God. She supports me, not just when I'm winning, but when I'm weary. She doesn't just clap for me in public—she covers me in private.

She sees the man I am and speaks to the man I'm becoming. That's purpose. That's partnership. That's love.

The Echo of a Promise

Every now and then, I go back and reread the notes I wrote to myself before we met. The ones where I dared to believe that someone like her existed. The ones where I promised to prepare for the day we would meet. And every time I reread them, I smile.

Because I realize now: *I was in love with a person I'd never met.*

And that love was not foolish. It was faith. It was obedience. It was vision.

Now, every day I live that love. And it's more beautiful than I could've ever written.

Scriptural Reflection

"Love is patient, love is kind. It does not envy, it does not boast, it is not proud. It does not dishonor others, it is not self-seeking, it is not easily angered, it keeps no record of wrongs. Love does not delight in evil but rejoices with the truth. It always protects, always trusts, always hopes, always perseveres. Love never fails."

—1 Corinthians 13:4–8 (NIV)

This scripture isn't poetic fluff. It's a blueprint. A map for what love looks like when it's lived.

Love isn't just about good feelings—it's about godly fruit. It protects. It trusts. It hopes. It perseveres.

And when God authors the love story, that love never fails.

So here I am—not just married, but walking in answered prayer. And to anyone still waiting, still believing, still preparing: don't give up.

The one you're praying for is worth the wait.

And if you do it God's way, you won't just fall in love—you'll *live* in it.

This is the story I waited a lifetime to live and spent years writing. And now, with the final sentence written about my journey of faith and fulfillment, I lay down the pen—knowing the Author of my life has already scripted the next masterpiece.

7 Biblical Principles for Finding True Love

A Practical Guide for Singles Who Believe God Has Someone for Them

These seven principles are not theories. They are truths drawn from Scripture, forged in my own story, and proven in the waiting. Each one is both a conviction to live by and a practice to walk out. If you take nothing else from this book, let these seven shape your journey.

1. Delight in the Lord First

> "Delight yourself in the Lord, and He will
> give you the desires of your heart."
> —Psalm 37:4

True love starts with true worship. Before you pursue a person, pursue God. Your relationship with Him is the foundation for every other relationship. When you put Him first, He aligns your desires with His plan.

Action Step: Instead of asking, *"When will I meet the one?"*, begin asking, *"Am I becoming the one God has called me to be?"*

2. Choose Purpose Over Preference

"Do not be unequally yoked with unbelievers."
—2 Corinthians 6:14

Looks fade. Chemistry cools. But purpose sustains. When choosing a partner, don't just ask, *"Do we click?"* Ask, *"Do we share vision, values, and faith?"* The wrong partner can derail your destiny, but the right one will multiply it.

Action Step: Write down your top 5 non-negotiable values. Pray for a partner who reflects them—and refuse to compromise when temptation comes.

3. Prepare Before You Pair

"Go to the ant, you sluggard; consider its ways and be wise!"
—Proverbs 6:6

Marriage magnifies what you bring into it. Debt, brokenness, unhealed wounds—they don't disappear after a wedding. Preparation is love in advance. Work on your finances, your healing, your spiritual growth. The greatest gift you can give your spouse is a whole you.

Action Step: List three areas of your life that need strengthening (spiritual, financial, emotional). Commit to practical steps this month to grow in each.

4. Guard Your Purity

"How can a young man keep his way pure? By guarding it according to your word."
—Psalm 119:9

Purity isn't about punishment—it's about preservation. It's protecting the beauty of intimacy for its rightful place. Like Joseph resisting Potiphar's wife, say "no" today so you can say "yes" tomorrow with no regrets.

Action Step: Set clear boundaries now. Decide in advance what lines you won't cross—and communicate them without apology.

5. Discern Before You Date

"By their fruit you will recognize them."
—Matthew 7:16

Attraction can blind, but character always reveals itself. Don't rush into emotional or physical intimacy. Watch from a distance first. Who are they when no one's looking? How do they treat people who can't help them? Time is the test of truth.

Action Step: Before saying yes to a date, observe. Pray. Ask: *Does their fruit confirm their faith?*

6. Trust God's Timing

"He has made everything beautiful in its time."
—Ecclesiastes 3:11

Waiting isn't wasted—it's refining. Culture says you're behind if you're not married by a certain age. God says you're right on time when your heart is aligned with His. Stop watching the clock and start watching His hand.

Action Step: When anxiety rises, write down three ways God has been faithful in your past. Let His record silence your rush.

7. Love Like Christ

*"Love is patient, love is kind. It does not envy,
it does not boast, it is not proud."*

—1 Corinthians 13:4

The world chases feelings; God commands love. Real love isn't about butterflies—it's about sacrifice. It's choosing to serve, forgive, and stay, even when it's hard. The way you practice love now—toward family, friends, even strangers—is training for how you will love your spouse.

Action Step: Each week, practice one act of sacrificial love (serve, forgive, encourage, give). You're not just waiting for love—you're becoming love.

Final Word

You don't find true love by accident—you prepare for it by faith. These principles are not just about meeting "the one." They're about becoming the one. If you live them, you won't just stumble into love; you'll recognize it, honor it, and sustain it for a lifetime.

Work With Jeremy

This book is just the beginning—now let's work together. If you're ready to take the next step, here's how I can help you:

- **Book Me for Your Next Conference or Event** – Bring a powerful, faith-driven message to inspire and transform your audience.
- **Hire Me as a Relationship Consultant** – Let's walk through the principles of finding and preparing for the person God has designed for you.
- **Hire Me for Business Consulting** – Unlock growth, leadership, and vision to take your business to the next level.

Take action today: **Visit JeremySanford.com to book me directly. Or email me at info@jeremysanford.com**

Your Free Gift

I want to thank you for investing in this book by giving you something extra:

A Free Guide: "5 Keys to Recognizing the Person God Has for You."

Here's how to claim it:

1. **Book a discovery call with me at JeremySanford.com.**
2. After our call, you'll receive the guide absolutely free.

www.ingramcontent.com/pod-product-compliance
Lightning Source LLC
Chambersburg PA
CBHW071003160426
43193CB00012B/1894